GRADE 2

Reader's and Writer's JOURNAL

Savvas Learning Company LLC, 15 East Midland Avenue, Paramus, NJ 07652

ISBN-13: 978-0-328-85157-7
ISBN-10: 0-328-85157-4
22 22

Table of Contents

Unit 6 Changing the World

Name Valentina

Short Vowels

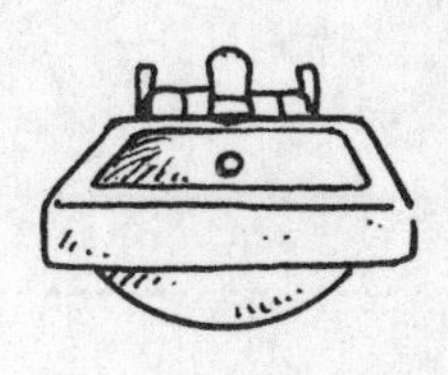

sing dock king clock sink

Say the word for each picture. **Write a, e, i, o,** or **u** to finish each word. Then **circle** the word that completes each sentence.

1. 

b__nk

2. 

r__ng

3. 

s__ck

4. 

n__ck

5. 

d__ck

6. 

tr__ck

7. 

w_ng

8. 

r__ck

9. Jan can __________ the ball. kick pocket picnic

10. Tim gives Jan a __________. sing ring nose

Children apply grade-level phonics and word analysis skills.

Name ______________________

Benchmark Vocabulary

DIRECTIONS Write sentences using the words below.

shade plastic spade shadow

Write in Response to Reading

DIRECTIONS Reread p. 4 of *Trouble at the Sandbox*. Who was making a river for the volcano? Use text evidence to support your answer.

Children demonstrate contextual understanding of Benchmark Vocabulary. Children read text closely and use text evidence in their written answers.

Writing

Name ________________________________

DIRECTIONS Reread pp. 2–5 of *Trouble at the Sandbox*. Write a paragraph about how Theo might respond to a classmate other than Izzy or Josh. Use key details from the text to help you.

Conventions

Identify Nouns Circle the nouns in the sentences below.

1. The grass was wet.
2. The sandbox is full of fresh sand.
3. Izzy wanted to dig a tunnel!
4. The girl peered through the door.
5. My classmate built a bridge during recess.

Children write routinely for a range of tasks, purposes, and audiences. Children practice various conventions of standard English.

Name ________________________

Benchmark Vocabulary

DIRECTIONS Write sentences using the words below.

scared carrying upset

Write in Response to Reading

DIRECTIONS Reread p. 7 of *Trouble at the Sandbox*. Write a sentence that tells why Josh looked like he was going to cry. Use examples from the text to support your answer.

Children demonstrate contextual understanding of Benchmark Vocabulary. Children read text closely and use text evidence in their written answers.

Name ______________________________

DIRECTIONS Using text evidence, answer the following questions about pp. 6–8 of *Trouble at the Sandbox.*

1. What happens first on p. 6?

2. What happens next?

3. On p. 7, what happens after Josh tells the older boys that they need the trucks?

4. List two events that take place on p. 8.

Children analyze and respond to literary and informational text.

Name ______________________

Writing

DIRECTIONS Create a classmate that will interact with the big boys. Write a paragraph that explains how the big boys would respond to that classmate. How would that classmate interact with the big boys? Use details from pp. 6–8 of *Trouble at the Sandbox* to support your paragraph.

Conventions

Capitalize Proper Nouns Circle the proper nouns that should be capitalized.

1. monica lives in a city called portland.
2. theo enjoys playing in the sandbox.
3. They went to tell Ms. lee everything that happened.
4. izzy was upset because the older boys were mean to them.
5. The big boy laughed at Theo and josh.

Children write routinely for a range of tasks, purposes, and audiences. Children practice various conventions of standard English.

Benchmark Vocabulary

Name ______________________________

DIRECTIONS Write sentences using the words below.

breath calm searched

Write in Response to Reading

DIRECTIONS Reread p. 10 of *Trouble at the Sandbox*. How does Theo feel about Ms. Lee? How do you know? Use evidence from the text to support your answer.

Children demonstrate contextual understanding of Benchmark Vocabulary. Children read text closely and use text evidence in their written answers.

Name ____________________

Sleuth Work

The Hunt for Amelia's Ring

"Janine, have you seen my ring?" Amelia asked.

Janine *had* seen her sister's ring. She had tried it on, but it was a little big, so she took it off . . . but where did she put it? Janine couldn't remember!

When she told her sister the truth, Amelia was upset. Janine had to find that ring! She crawled under tables, peeked inside dresser drawers, looked behind the couch, and opened every cabinet. Finally, she gave up and went outside to sit on the front steps.

Her neighbor, Mrs. Kim, came up the steps "I find it useful to retrace my steps when I can't find something," Mrs. Kim said.

Janine thought and thought. First, she had done homework, and then she had eaten a snack. Then . . . aha! She remembered!

Janine helped carry Mrs. Kim's groceries. Then she ran to her apartment and went to the kitchen windowsill. There it was! The ring was right where Janine had left it when she helped water Mom's plants. Janine ran to give it to Amelia. She had learned her lesson about taking what wasn't hers. She also learned that two heads are better than one when there is a mystery to solve!

Children read text closely to determine what the text says.

Name ______________________________

Look for Clues

Underline the text that tells how Mrs. Kim helped Janine.

Look for Clues: Extend Your Ideas

What did Janine do once Mrs. Kim gave her that tip?

____

Ask Questions

Write a question that you might ask someone who has lost something.

____

Ask Questions: Extend Your Ideas

Ask a question that you might follow up with if the person found the lost item.

____

Make Your Case

Underline the text that tells how Amelia reacted to Janine losing her ring. Then underline the text that tells how Janine reacted when she found the ring.

Make Your Case: Extend Your Ideas

Identify one lesson Janine learned. Write the lesson on a sheet of paper.

Children read text closely to determine what the text says.

Name ______________________________

Writing

DIRECTIONS You will create a character who will be a friend of Theo's. Use the graphic organizer to help you list your character's physical traits, thoughts, and word choices. Write a paragraph using the information from the web. Be sure to include Theo's point of view of the character. On a separate piece of paper, draw a picture of the character to illustrate your description.

Conventions

Plural Nouns Underline the plural nouns.

1. day	farmers	boots	spider	animals
2. sand	boy	teacher	trucks	friends
3. box	volcanoes	cats	school	arms
4. cup	keyboard	books	computer	mouse

Children write routinely for a range of tasks, purposes, and audiences. Children practice various conventions of standard English.

Name ______________________

Benchmark Vocabulary

DIRECTIONS Write sentences using the words below.

shrugged tipped awesome sank

Write in Response to Reading

DIRECTIONS Reread p. 14 of *Trouble at the Sandbox*. How does Theo feel when he turns around and sees that the big boy is behind him again? Use examples from the text to support your answer.

Children demonstrate contextual understanding of Benchmark Vocabulary. Children read text closely and use text evidence in their written answers.

Name ______________________

Reading Analysis

DIRECTIONS Using evidence from the text, answer the following questions about pp. 12–14 of *Trouble at the Sandbox*.

1. List three events that happened on pp. 12–14.

2. How does Izzy feel when she sees the volcano?

3. What does Izzy do after Josh fills the truck with water?

Children analyze and respond to literary and informational text.

Name ____________________

Writing

DIRECTIONS Choose a character from *Trouble at the Sandbox* and create a new character. Imagine an event that your new character and the character from the text will have different points of view about. Then write a narrative using dialogue that shows these differing points of view.

Conventions

Irregular Plural Nouns Cross out the irregular plural nouns.

1. children	birds	sheep	mice	bugs
2. teeth	buses	people	hats	dogs
3. cups	men	rabbits	loaves	desks
4. cows	geese	crows	wolves	gerbils

Children write routinely for a range of tasks, purposes, and audiences. Children practice various conventions of standard English.

Benchmark Vocabulary

Name ______________________________

DIRECTIONS Write sentences using the words below.

bravely background

Write in Response to Reading

DIRECTIONS Reread p. 16 of *Trouble at the Sandbox*. How does Ms. Lee's point of view change? Why? Use evidence from the text to support your answer.

Children demonstrate contextual understanding of Benchmark Vocabulary. Children read text closely and use text evidence in their written answers.

Name ______________________

DIRECTIONS Using evidence from pp. 15–18 of *Trouble at the Sandbox,* follow the directions below.

1. On the lines below, write the names of two characters. Then consider each character's point of view on a topic discussed in the text.

Character 1:

Character 2:

2. Tell the point of view on a topic for Character 1.

3. Tell the point of view on a topic for Character 2.

Children analyze and respond to literary and informational text.

Name ______________________

Writing

DIRECTIONS Revisit pp. 15–18 of *Trouble at the Sandbox.* Draw a picture of the sandbox on a separate piece of paper. Show who is there and what is happening. Then rewrite the scene in a paragraph. Use descriptive details to show what each character did and said.

Conventions

Collective Nouns Circle the collective nouns.

1. community insects herd cows gosling
2. marker army buses committee pod
3. bouquet sweep swarm sequence ants
4. cellphones group brooms team department

Children write routinely for a range of tasks, purposes, and audiences. Children practice various conventions of standard English.

Name ______________________________

Long Vowels Spelled VCe

face

mice

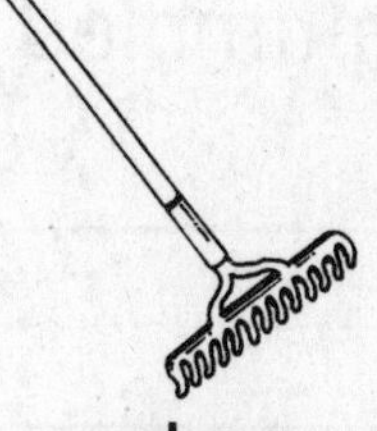
rake

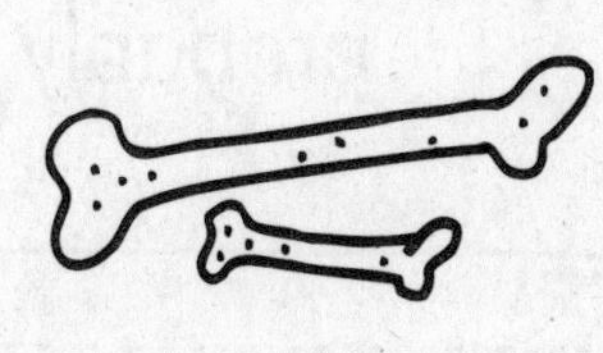
bone

Say the word for each picture.
Write a, e, i, o, or **u** to finish each word.

1. 
c __ ge

2. 
r __ se

3. 
r __ ce

4. 
sp __ ce

5. 
sn __ ke

6. 
sl __ ce

7. 
h __ se

8. 
t __ pe

Find the word that has the same middle sound as the picture.
Mark the space to show your answer.

9. 
love

swarm

dive

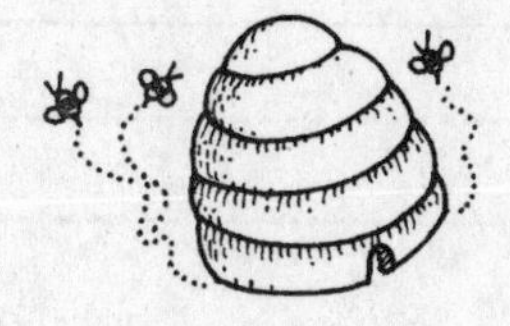

10. mule

beam

stripe

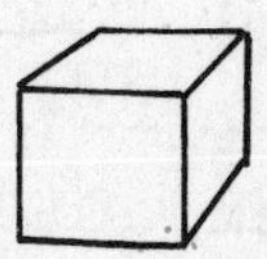

Children apply grade-level phonics and word analysis skills.

Name ______________________________

Benchmark Vocabulary

DIRECTIONS Write sentences using the words below.

probably   mumbled   properly   nodded

Write in Response to Reading

DIRECTIONS Reread p. 20 of *Trouble at the Sandbox*. How does the picture on this page help you understand what's happening in the story?

Children demonstrate contextual understanding of Benchmark Vocabulary. Children read text closely and use text evidence in their written answers.

Name ______________________________

DIRECTIONS Look at the description and picture you created for your new character in Lesson 3. Think about the scene when Theo meets this new character. Write a short paragraph or scene that would be the beginning of a chapter about Theo and the new character. Use information you have learned about writing a strong beginning.

Verbs in the Present and Past Tense Circle the present-tense verbs. Underline the past-tense verbs.

1.	swim	eats	jumped	walked	smiles
2.	run	hopped	jump	jogged	volunteered
3.	wish	smiled	snowed	rains	trained
4.	ran	published	turns	writes	sprinted

Children write routinely for a range of tasks, purposes, and audiences. Children practice various conventions of standard English.

Name ______________________

Benchmark Vocabulary

DIRECTIONS Write a sentence using the word below.

corner

Write in Response to Reading

DIRECTIONS Reread p. 24 of *Trouble at the Sandbox*. Why does Theo hand Ben a truck? What happened in the story that changed the relationship between Theo and Ben? Use examples from the text to support your answer.

Children demonstrate contextual understanding of Benchmark Vocabulary. Children read text closely and use text evidence in their written answers.

Name ______________________________

DIRECTIONS Using evidence from the text, answer the following questions about pp. 22–24 of *Trouble at the Sandbox*.

1. Reread the last paragraph on p. 22. Why does Theo's heart sink?

2. How has Ben's point of view changed since Chapter 1?

3. List two events from the text that show how Theo's point of view about Ben has changed.

Children analyze and respond to literary and informational text.

Name ______________________________

Writing

DIRECTIONS Recall the events in *Trouble at the Sandbox,* beginning with the discovery that Ben and his friends have been taking the trucks to make a movie. List three or four major events in chronological order. Then write a paragraph recounting the events in the second half of the text. Use both types of sequence words when writing your paragraph.

Conventions

Use Simple Sentences Circle the subject in each sentence.

1. Izzy ran into the sandbox.
2. The volcano was bigger than before!
3. The teacher will help the students.
4. Theo ran toward the sandbox!

Children write routinely for a range of tasks, purposes, and audiences.
Children practice various conventions of standard English.

Benchmark Vocabulary

Name ____________________________

DIRECTIONS Write a sentence using the words below.

tumbling vanished ambling

Write in Response to Reading

DIRECTIONS Reread pp. 5–7 of *Snowshoe Hare's Winter Home*. Pick one animal that Snowshoe Hare talked with. Write a sentence that tells what Snowshoe Hare thinks about that animal's plan for surviving winter. Use the text to support your answer.

Children demonstrate contextual understanding of Benchmark Vocabulary. Children read text closely and use text evidence in their written answers.

Name ______________________________

Writing

DIRECTIONS Expand on the story you started in Lesson 6 using characters from *Trouble at the Sandbox* and your new character from Lesson 3. Then review the story and decide on one additional event to add to your story. Use details to describe actions, thoughts, and feelings.

Conventions

Identify Irregular Verbs Circle the irregular verbs.

1. At last Snowshoe Hare saw the creature in the doorway.
2. The animals ran out to the road.
3. The creature built his winter shelter.
4. We met at the sandbox to build another volcano.

Children write routinely for a range of tasks, purposes, and audiences. Children practice various conventions of standard English.

Name ______________________________

Benchmark Vocabulary

DIRECTIONS Write sentences using the words below.

nibbling thumped crackled

Write in Response to Reading

DIRECTIONS In what ways are the settings of *Trouble at the Sandbox* and *Snowshoe Hare's Winter Home* different? Tell at least two ways that they are not the same. Use the text to support your answer.

Children demonstrate contextual understanding of Benchmark Vocabulary. Children read text closely and use text evidence in their written answers.

Name ____________________________

DIRECTIONS Revisit pp. 5–10 of *Snowshoe Hare's Winter Home*. Think about the plot, or what happened, in this chapter. Then list the major events in the chapter in order below.

1. ____________________________

2. ____________________________

3. ____________________________

4. ____________________________

5. ____________________________

Children analyze and respond to literary and informational text.

Writing

Name ______________________

DIRECTIONS Recall a sequence of events from *Snowshoe Hare's Winter Home* that you want to retell. Write one paragraph about a sequence of at least three events. Use words that tell *when* to support your answer.

Conventions

Identify Irregular Verbs Circle the correct past-tense verb.

1. The truck (comed, came) to a stop.
2. He (sprang, springed) from the table.
3. The high winds (blew, blewed) snow around the playground.
4. The snows melted and the grass (became, becomed) visible again.

Children write routinely for a range of tasks, purposes, and audiences. Children practice various conventions of standard English.

Name ______________________

Benchmark Vocabulary

DIRECTIONS Write sentences using the words below.

speck peering bounded

Write in Response to Reading

DIRECTIONS Revisit pp. 11–13 of *Snowshoe Hare's Winter Home*. How do the illustrations help you understand the story? Use examples from the text to support your answer.

Children demonstrate contextual understanding of Benchmark Vocabulary. Children read text closely and use text evidence in their written answers.

Name ______________________________

DIRECTIONS Using evidence from the text, answer the following questions about pp. 11–13 of *Snowshoe Hare's Winter Home.*

1. Revisit the second paragraph on p. 11. What word best supports the illustration?

2. Revisit the third paragraph on p. 11. Where have Snowshoe Hare's friends gone?

3. Revisit p. 12. Is Snowshoe Hare still alone? Who does he see?

Children analyze and respond to literary and informational text.

Name ____________________

Writing

DIRECTIONS Write a draft of the story you began planning in previous lessons.

Conventions

Irregular Verbs Write the correct past-tense form of each verb below.

1. weaves ____________

2. leaps ____________

3. hangs ____________

4. fall ____________

Children write routinely for a range of tasks, purposes, and audiences. Children practice various conventions of standard English.

Name ______________________________

Long Vowels Spelled VCe

smil_e_

dim_e_

pil_e_

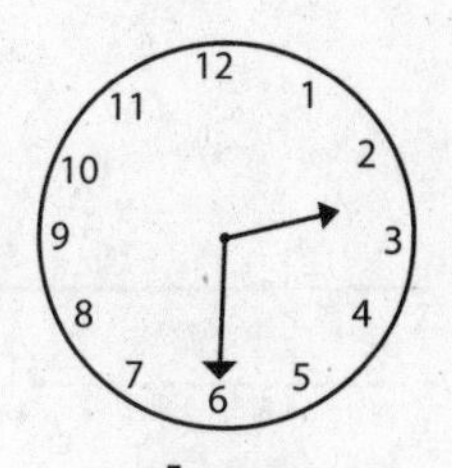

tim_e_

Say the word for each picture.
Write a, e, i, o, or **u** to finish each word.

1. 

m__le

2. 

sl__ce

3. 

m__ce

4. 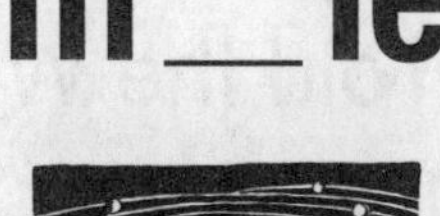

sp__ce

5. 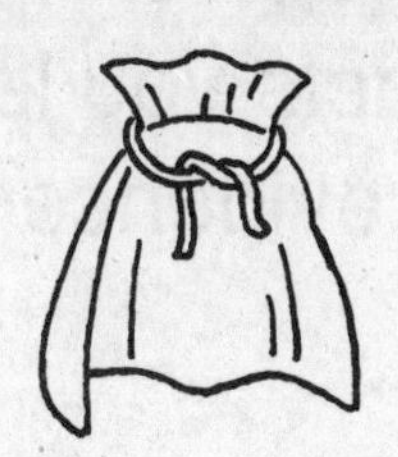

c__pe

6. 

gr__pe

Find the word that has the same middle sound as the picture.
Mark the space to show your answer.

7. hose

cart 

mule

8. mug 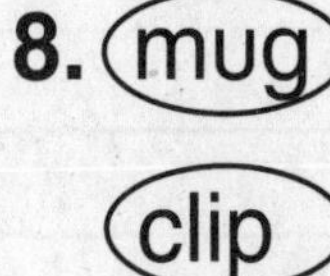

clip

bite 

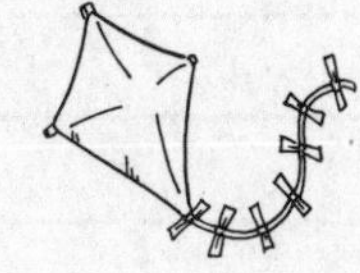

Children apply grade-level phonics and word analysis skills.

Name ______________________________

Benchmark Vocabulary

DIRECTIONS Write sentences using the words below.

frost orchards amber

Write in Response to Reading

DIRECTIONS Revisit the poem "Something Told the Wild Geese." What are two facts you learn about geese by reading the poem? Use evidence from the poem to support your answer.

Children demonstrate contextual understanding of Benchmark Vocabulary. Children read text closely and use text evidence in their written answers.

Writing

Name ______________________

DIRECTIONS Revise the draft of the story you have been working on. Review your introduction, paragraphs, sentences, and conclusion. Make notes about where changes are needed as you review.

Conventions

Pronouns Circle the pronouns in the sentences below. Then write a sentence of your own using a pronoun.

1. He was cold.
2. She liked the snow.
3. They read a poem about geese.
4. ______________________

Children write routinely for a range of tasks, purposes, and audiences. Children practice various conventions of standard English.

Name ____________________

Benchmark Vocabulary

DIRECTIONS Write sentences using the words below.

sharing scared vanished

Write in Response to Reading

DIRECTIONS Think about the characters in *Trouble at the Sandbox* and *Snowshoe Hare's Winter Home.* Which character's point of view do you most agree with? Use examples from the text to support your answer.

Children demonstrate contextual understanding of Benchmark Vocabulary. Children read text closely and use text evidence in their written answers.

Name ______________________

DIRECTIONS Using evidence from *Trouble at the Sandbox* and *Snowshoe Hare's Winter Home,* follow the directions below.

1. Name two characters from *Trouble at the Sandbox* or *Snowshoe Hare's Winter Home* that have different points of view.

Character 1: ______________________

Character 2: ______________________

2. Tell the point of view on a topic for Character 1.

3. Tell the point of view on a topic for Character 2.

Children analyze and respond to literary and informational text.

Name ______________________

Writing

DIRECTIONS Edit the draft of the new story you have worked on in previous lessons. Check capitalization, punctuation, spelling, and grammar. Review the title, author name, and paragraph indentation. Use a colored pen or pencil to mark changes.

Conventions

Pronouns Write the correct pronoun in the blank.

1. He leaped back as water splashed ________.

2. Snowshoe Hare will spend the winter with ________.

3. Ms. Lee is a nice teacher. ________ voice is always relaxed.

4. The big boys were mean to Theo. Then ________ walked away.

Children write routinely for a range of tasks, purposes, and audiences. Children practice various conventions of standard English.

Name ______________________

DIRECTIONS Write sentences using the words below.

probably snuggle

Write in Response to Reading

DIRECTIONS What happens at the end of *Trouble at the Sandbox*? How do things change for Theo, Izzy, and Josh? Use examples from the text to support your answer.

Children demonstrate contextual understanding of Benchmark Vocabulary. Children read text closely and use text evidence in their written answers.

Name ______________________________

A Birthday Surprise

"Mom will be so surprised!" Sadie said. She looked proudly at the cake that Uncle Curt had helped her and her brother Sam make for Mom's birthday.

"Let's put it in the dining room," Sam said. "That way it will be the first thing Mom sees."

Sadie agreed, and Sam carefully picked it up. Then trouble arrived. Their cousin Wes bounded through the swinging door. The door bumped the plate, the plate tipped, and splat! The cake landed on the floor.

"Oh, no!" Sadie cried. "What can we do now?"

"We'll have to be creative," Sam said.

Uncle Curt had made them pancakes that morning before he left for work, and they still had leftovers. "We can't give Mom a birthday cake. Let's give her birthday pancakes instead!" Sadie said.

"Great idea!" said Sam. They warmed the pancakes. Sam spread jam on each one. Then Sadie put on banana slices. They stacked the pancakes and put candles on the top.

Children read text closely to determine what the text says.

Name ______________________________

Just then, they heard Mom coming down the stairs. Sam raced to the stairs and asked her to stay in her bedroom. Mom thought there might be a surprise. Then Sadie arrived with the birthday pancakes. Mom laughed. “How did you know that I have always wanted to have a birthday breakfast in bed?” she said.

Look for Clues
Underline the text that tells about Sadie’s talents and personality.

Ask Questions
Write a question that you might ask someone who has had to fix a problem quickly.

____

Make Your Case
Underline the first major event. Then underline the next major event.

Make Your Case: Extend Your Ideas
Explain why sequence is important in a story. Use examples from this story.

____

____

Children read text closely to determine what the text says.

Name ______________________________

Writing

Type your story on a computer and print it out. Follow these steps:

- Open and save your document.
- Add the story title and your name at the top of the page.
- Make your editing corrections as you type.
- Read your document to make sure you made all the corrections and that you did not make any typing mistakes.
- Print your document and read it one last time.

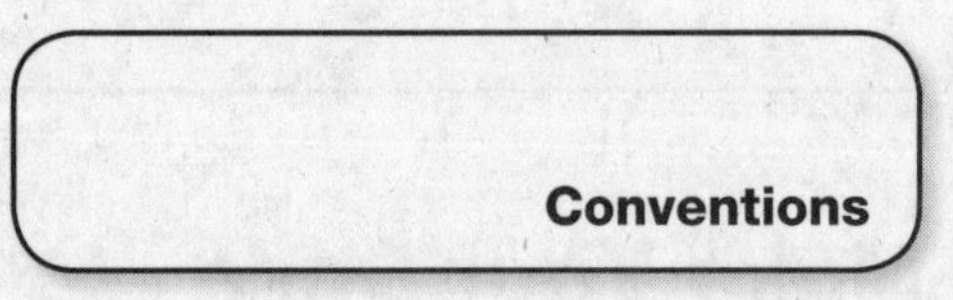

Conventions

Reflexive Pronouns Circle the reflexive pronoun in each sentence.

1. I like myself.
2. "Take a look at yourself!" they said.
3. We can make the volcano ourselves.
4. I wish the big boys would play among themselves.

Children write routinely for a range of tasks, purposes, and audiences. Children practice various conventions of standard English.

Name ______________________

Consonant Blends

Say the word for each picture.
Pick the letters from the box that finish each word.

bl	sl	nt	cl	nd	sk	st	str	fr	spl

1. 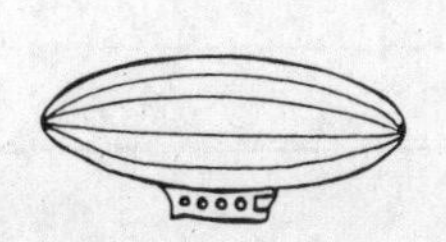
2. 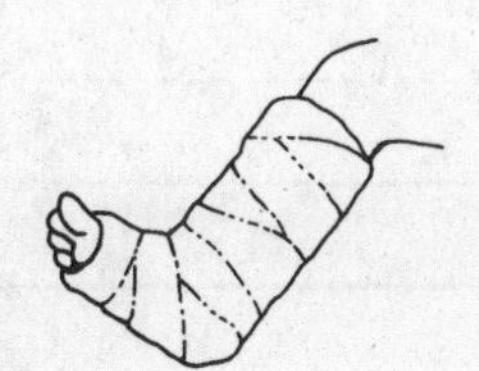
3. 
4. 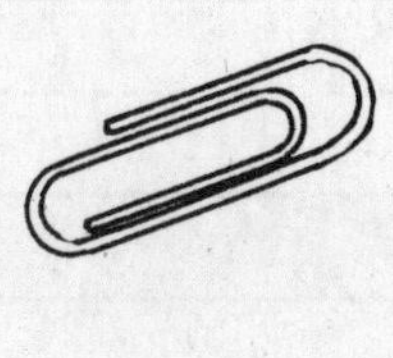

____imp ____ca ____ma ____ip

Read each sentence. **Add** the missing letters to the word or words. **Use** the box above for help.

5. My ______ iend Sam and I put up a te ______.

6. Our ______ eeping bags were on the grou ______.

7. They seemed to be on a ______ ant.

8. We ______ etched out on our backs.

9. I ______ ashed water on my face to ______ ay awake.

Children apply grade-level phonics and word analysis skills.

Name ______________________________

Benchmark Vocabulary

DIRECTIONS Write sentences using the words below.

exchange facts subway country

Write in Response to Reading

DIRECTIONS Revisit pp. 6–7 of *Friends Around the World*. Who is telling the story? Why are they telling the story? Use examples from the text to support your answer.

Children demonstrate contextual understanding of Benchmark Vocabulary. Children read text closely and use text evidence in their written answers.

Writing

Name ___________________________

DIRECTIONS Draw a picture of a rural area. Then write a caption for your picture.

Conventions

Identify Adjectives Adjectives describe nouns. Circle the adjectives in the sentences below.

1. The loud subway was Isabel's favorite part about going to school.
2. The elevator in her building was cold and unpleasant.
3. The big apartment building towered over the park.
4. Her motorcycle bounced up and down on the bumpy roads of Ho Chi Minh City.

Children write routinely for a range of tasks, purposes, and audiences.
Children practice various conventions of standard English.

Name ______________________________

Benchmark Vocabulary

DIRECTIONS Write sentences using the words below.

uniform parka outback

Write in Response to Reading

DIRECTIONS Revisit pp. 12–13 of *Friends Around the World*. What details does Dan provide that help you understand where he lives? Use examples from the text to support your answer.

Children demonstrate contextual understanding of Benchmark Vocabulary. Children read text closely and use text evidence in their written answers.

Name ______________________________

DIRECTIONS Look at the photos and captions on pp. 8–13 of *Friends Around the World*. Think about a photo you would like to add to one of these pages. Write a description of that photo and the caption that you would include with it. Which key details would this photo support?

Children analyze and respond to literary and informational text.

Name ______________________

Writing

DIRECTIONS Select one of the places mentioned in *Friends Around the World* and describe it using facts provided by the writer. Be sure to use adjectives in your description.

Conventions

Identifying Adjectives Complete the sentence by adding an adjective.

1. It was a ______________________ day, so Isabel stayed inside.

2. When I woke up it was ______________________, so my Mom made me put on a hat.

Children write routinely for a range of tasks, purposes, and audiences.
Children practice various conventions of standard English.

Benchmark Vocabulary

Name ______________________________

DIRECTIONS Write sentences using the words below.

favorite scored traditional

Write in Response to Reading

DIRECTIONS Revisit pp. 16–17 of *Friends Around the World.* What are Hau's favorite things to eat? Use examples from the text to support your answer.

Children demonstrate contextual understanding of Benchmark Vocabulary. Children read text closely and use text evidence in their written answers.

Name ____________________

DIRECTIONS Using the text, answer the following questions about pp. 14–17 of *Friends Around the World.*

1. What is the main idea on pp. 14–15?

2. List two details that support the main idea.

3. What is the main idea on pp. 16–17?

4. List two details that support the main idea.

Children analyze and respond to literary and informational text.

Name ______________________________

DIRECTIONS Look over the list the class made about pp. 14–17 of *Friends Around the World*. Choose one of these topics and write a list of questions about the topic that you want answered.

Adjectives Read the paragraph. Circle the adjectives.

One sunny day, I went to a baseball game. Soon the yellow sun peeked out from behind the clouds. My favorite team wore white uniforms with black stripes. Before long, I had two delicious hot dogs to eat!

Children write routinely for a range of tasks, purposes, and audiences.
Children practice various conventions of standard English.

Name ______________________

Benchmark Vocabulary

DIRECTIONS Write sentences using the words below.

frozen meal caribou

Write in Response to Reading

DIRECTIONS Revisit pp. 18–19 of *Friends Around the World*. What does Akiak's father do that he wants to do when he gets older? Use examples from the text to support your answer.

Children demonstrate contextual understanding of Benchmark Vocabulary. Children read text closely and use text evidence in their written answers.

Name ________________________________

Writing

DIRECTIONS Write a paragraph in which you identify the author's purpose in *Friends Around the World*. Use details from the text to support your answer.

Conventions

Identifying Adjectives Write your own sentences using adjectives from *Friends Around the World*.

1. ________________________________

2. ________________________________

3. ________________________________

Children write routinely for a range of tasks, purposes, and audiences. Children practice various conventions of standard English.

Benchmark Vocabulary

Name ______________________________

DIRECTIONS Write sentences using the words below.

seasons pours floods

Write in Response to Reading

DIRECTIONS Revisit pp. 24–25 of *Friends Around the World*. How does the picture on this page support the words? Use details from the text to support your answer.

Children demonstrate contextual understanding of Benchmark Vocabulary. Children read text closely and use text evidence in their written answers.

Name ______________________________

DIRECTIONS Look at the photos and captions on pp. 22–25 of *Friends Around the World*. For each page, write the page number and then a sentence that tells what you learned from the photo and caption on that page.

Children analyze and respond to literary and informational text.

Name ______________________

Writing

DIRECTIONS Revisit pp. 24–25 of *Friends Around the World.* Then write a paragraph using facts about Ho Chi Minh City. Use evidence from the text to support your answer.

Conventions

Review Adjectives Replace each bold print adjective with a new adjective.

1. I wore my **wooly** sweater today.

2. We had **sweet** fruit for dessert.

3. It's always very **warm** in Ho Chi Minh City.

Children write routinely for a range of tasks, purposes, and audiences. Children practice various conventions of standard English.

Name ______________________

Endings *-s, -ed, -ing*

talk talk**s** lift lift**ing** drop drop**ped** smile smil**ing**

Use the word in ( ) to finish each sentence.
Add ***-s, -ed,* or *-ing*** to make a word.
Write the new word on the line.

1. Isabel ______________ Dad. (hug)

2. Mom ______________ good-bye. (wave)

3. Isabel ______________ her hat and went to school. (grab)

4. This is an ______________ day. (excite)

5. Akiak and his dad are going ______________. (fish)

Children apply grade-level phonics and word analysis skills.

Name ______________________

Benchmark Vocabulary

DIRECTIONS Write sentences using the words below.

bandage barbecue

Write in Response to Reading

DIRECTIONS Revisit pp. 28–29 of *Friends Around the World*. What is the purpose of the Royal Flying Doctor Service? Why couldn't Dan's mom drive him to the hospital? Use examples from the text to support your answer.

Children demonstrate contextual understanding of Benchmark Vocabulary. Children read text closely and use text evidence in their written answers.

Writing

Name ______________________________

DIRECTIONS Choose one of the children that you have read about in *Friends Around the World*. Write about what that child does using key words to help you describe them. Use details from the text to help you write your response.

Conventions

Adverbs Circle the adverb in each sentence.

1. Dan softly caressed his chicken.
2. Tomorrow Grandpa will come for a visit.
3. It snowed heavily, so they closed the school.
4. Dan hurt his leg, but he will be better soon.

Children write routinely for a range of tasks, purposes, and audiences. Children practice various conventions of standard English.

Name ______________________________

Benchmark Vocabulary

DIRECTIONS Write sentences using the words below.

learned   common   activities   exciting

Write in Response to Reading

DIRECTIONS Revisit p. 30 of *Friends Around the World*. What does Isabel say she has in common with her new friends? Use details from the text to support your answer.

Children demonstrate contextual understanding of Benchmark Vocabulary. Children read text closely and use text evidence in their written answers.

Name ______________________________

DIRECTIONS Revisit pp. 30–32 of *Friends Around the World*. How does the glossary help you understand the text? Use examples from the text to support your answer.

Children analyze and respond to literary and informational text.

Name ______________________

Writing

DIRECTIONS Think about the two cities that you read about in *Friends Around the World*—New York City and Ho Chi Minh City. Write a few sentences that tell how these cities are alike and different. Use linking words to connect your ideas about each city.

____

____

____

____

Conventions

Adverbs Add an adverb to each sentence.

1. The girls will go swimming ______________________

______________________.

2. Akiak ______________________

______________________ closed the door behind her.

Children write routinely for a range of tasks, purposes, and audiences. Children practice various conventions of standard English.

Benchmark Vocabulary

Name ______________________________

DIRECTIONS Write sentences using the words below.

mighty fierce

Write in Response to Reading

DIRECTIONS Before Chrissy and Jenny lived at 107 Maple Street, other people lived on the land. Tell how these other people lived on the land before there was a house built on it. Use details from the text to support your answer.

Children demonstrate contextual understanding of Benchmark Vocabulary. Children read text closely and use text evidence in their written answers.

Name ______________________________

Unlikely Friends

Every Monday afternoon, Anya helped Ms. Hickson with her yardwork. Ms. Hickson always watched Anya from her tall porch. She even had a glass of juice waiting for her when the work was done. Anya often brought along her violin. Ms. Hickson would beam with delight when Anya played for her. Anya used to complain about visiting Ms. Hickson, but Anya's mother always insisted she go. She said that neighbors should take care of each other.

One Monday, Anya came without her violin. When she finished raking the yard, she sat down sadly beside her neighbor. Ms. Hickson asked what had happened. Anya burst into tears. Her brother had broken her violin by accident. There was no way it could be fixed in time for her fall concert. Ms. Hickson disappeared into the house. She returned a few minutes later with an old violin case. Inside was the most beautiful violin Anya had ever seen. Ms. Hickson picked it up lovingly and handed it to Anya. Anya played a few notes, laid the violin in its velvet-lined case, and threw her arms around Ms. Hickson. The violin was the best gift Anya had ever received.

Children read text closely to determine what the text says.

Name ______________________________

Look for Clues

Underline the text that tells how Anya and Ms. Hickson were good neighbors.

Look for Clues: Extend Your Ideas

What word tells you how important the violin was to Ms. Hickson? Circle it.

Ask Questions

Write two questions you might ask Ms. Hickson if you were visiting her.

Make Your Case

Underline the text that supports what we know about the relationship between Anya and Ms. Hickson.

Make Your Case: Extend Your Ideas

Circle the text that tells how Anya used to feel about Ms. Hickson.

Children read text closely to determine what the text says.

Name ______________________________

Writing

DIRECTIONS On a separate sheet of paper, draw a picture of a rural setting from *The House on Maple Street*. Then write a paragraph that introduces the time period, gives several details about the setting, and concludes by telling why the time period is important.

____

____

____

____

____

____

Conventions

Adverbs Underline the adverbs in the sentences below. Then write your own sentence using an adverb.

1. The rabbits suddenly jumped out of the bushes.
2. After reading *The House on Maple Street*, I wondered what the area near my house will look like in the future.

   ____

3. ______________________________

Children write routinely for a range of tasks, purposes, and audiences. Children practice various conventions of standard English.

Benchmark Vocabulary

Name ______________________________

DIRECTIONS Write sentences using the words below.

snug complained

Write in Response to Reading

DIRECTIONS Write your opinion about whether the changes made by the people at 107 Maple Street were good or bad. Use examples from the text to support your thoughts.

Children demonstrate contextual understanding of Benchmark Vocabulary. Children read text closely and use text evidence in their written answers.

Name ______________________

DIRECTIONS Revisit pp. 14–16 of *The House on Maple Street.* How does the author use language to show that the location is the same, but the time is different? How do the visuals in the story help you understand what is taking place and when?

Children analyze and respond to literary and informational text.

Writing

Name ______________________________

DIRECTIONS Research the area around your home and how it has changed over time. Interview your parents or neighbors and ask about how the area around your home has changed over time. Then draw a picture on a separate sheet of paper showing how it looks now and write sentences describing the neighborhood as it looks today.

Conventions

Use Adverbs Circle the adverbs that tell *when* and *where*. Then write two sentences of your own that use one of the adverbs below.

1. Circle the adverbs that tell *when*.

   yesterday slowly sweetly daily later

2. Circle the adverbs that tell *where*.

   loudly behind around snowed soon

   ____

3. ______________________________

   ____

4. ______________________________

Children write routinely for a range of tasks, purposes, and audiences. Children practice various conventions of standard English.

Name ______________________________

Benchmark Vocabulary

DIRECTIONS Write sentences using the words below.

paved remained

Write in Response to Reading

DIRECTIONS Tell your opinion about whether you would want to live on Maple Street. Use details from the text to support your opinion.

Children demonstrate contextual understanding of Benchmark Vocabulary. Children read text closely and use text evidence in their written answers.

Name ______________________________

DIRECTIONS The story structure of *The House on Maple Street* begins in the present time. It then jumps back to 300 years ago. Readers then follow the story of this place until they read once again about present times.

Beginning with the events 300 years ago, make a list of 5 events that take place in chronological order. Include the page numbers where these events are found.

1. ______________________________

2. ______________________________

3. ______________________________

4. ______________________________

5. ______________________________

Children analyze and respond to literary and informational text.

Name ____________________

Writing

DIRECTIONS Using the information you learned from interviewing your parents or neighbors, draw a second picture of how your neighborhood looked in the past. Write sentences using descriptive details to explain your drawing. Then compare how your neighborhood is now to how it was in the past.

Conventions

Use Adverbs Complete the sentences below using adverbs.

1. The child ____________________ walked to school.

2. My sister ____________________ painted my fingernails.

Children write routinely for a range of tasks, purposes, and audiences.
Children practice various conventions of standard English.

Name ______________________

Endings *-s, -ed, -ing*

scream scream**s** cry cry**ing** slip slipp**ed** run runn**ing**

Use the word in ( ) to finish each sentence.
Add *-s, -ed,* or *-ing* to make a word.
Write the new word on the line.

1. Isabel ______________ to the subway because she was excited. (skip)

2. I hope we are there when she ______________ the prize. (win)

3. The little boy was ______________ because he injured his knee. (yell)

4. The frog ______________ out of the fox's way! (hop)

5. Hau sometimes liked to go ______________ after school. (swim)

Children apply grade-level phonics and word analysis skills.

Name ______________________

Benchmark Vocabulary

DIRECTIONS Write sentences using the words below.

cricket mighty

Write in Response to Reading

DIRECTIONS Revisit pp. 20–21 of *Friends Around the World* and pp. 34–35 of *The House on Maple Street*. Compare the illustrations in the two texts. Tell one way they are alike and one way they are different.

Children demonstrate contextual understanding of Benchmark Vocabulary. Children read text closely and use text evidence in their written answers.

Name ______________________

Writing

DIRECTIONS Refer to your drawings and your graphic organizers. Write a paragraph in which you compare and contrast the two homes. You should introduce your topic in the first sentence and conclude the paragraph in the last sentence.

Conventions

Contractions Rewrite the sentences below using contractions.

1. Juanita did not do her homework.

2. Scott has not played baseball in a long time.

Children write routinely for a range of tasks, purposes, and audiences.
Children practice various conventions of standard English.

Name ______________________

Benchmark Vocabulary

DIRECTIONS Write a sentence using the word below.

outback

Write in Response to Reading

DIRECTIONS Revisit pp. 32–33 of *The House on Maple Street* and pp. 12–13 of *Friends Around the World*. How is Dan's farm different from the farm in *The House on Maple Street*? Use examples from both texts to support your answer.

Children demonstrate contextual understanding of Benchmark Vocabulary. Children read text closely and use text evidence in their written answers.

Name ______________________________

DIRECTIONS Using examples from *The House on Maple Street* and *Friends Around the World*, choose two words and phrases from each text that help you understand what is happening. Then use each of those words and phrases in your own sentences.

1. The House on Maple Street:

2.

3. Friends Around the World:

4.

Children analyze and respond to literary and informational text.

Name ______________________

Writing

DIRECTIONS Revise the explanatory piece that you worked on in Lessons 10 and 11 using peer feedback. Edit your piece for spelling and capitalization. Then make a clean final copy to share. Use *Friends Around the World* and *The House on Maple Street* to look for ideas and examples.

Conventions

Contractions Rewrite the underlined words as contractions. Don't forget to use apostrophes. Then write a sentence of your own that uses a contraction.

1. She is reading us a good book. ____________

2. They have been painting the house. ____________

3. We would like to go to the zoo. ____________

4. ______________________________________

Children write routinely for a range of tasks, purposes, and audiences.
Children practice various conventions of standard English.

Name ______________________

Consonant Digraphs *ch, tch, sh, th, wh*

chicken watch ship thirty wheel

Say the word for each picture.
Write ch, tch, sh, th, or **wh** to finish each word.

1.  **2.**  **3.** 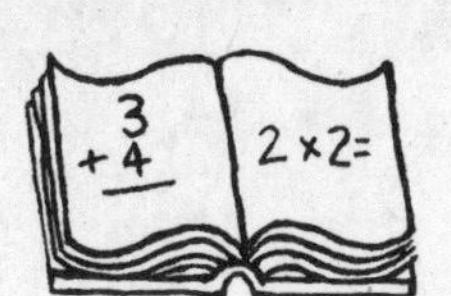

4. 

___**ale** **i**___ **ma**___ ___**erry**

5.  **6.**  **7.** 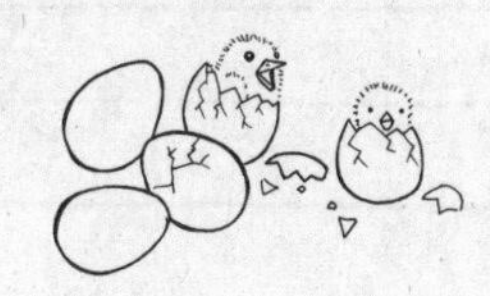 **8.** 

___**eep** **fi**___ **ha**___ **ba**___

Write a sentence using each word.

9. that ______________________

10. thrill ______________________.

Children apply grade-level phonics and word analysis skills.

Name ______________________________

Benchmark Vocabulary

DIRECTIONS Write a sentence using the word below.

save

Write in Response to Reading

DIRECTIONS Write several sentences about Alexander. What does he do, think, and feel? Use details from the text to support your answer.

Children demonstrate contextual understanding of Benchmark Vocabulary. Children read text closely and use text evidence in their written answers.

Name ______________________________

DIRECTIONS Write several sentences about the decisions Alexander made about spending his money. How does he react to his decisions? Revisit the text and illustrations to find examples of the decisions Alexander made.

Singular Possessives Circle the singular possessives. Then write your own sentences using singular possessives.

1. dogs'   sister's   friend's   girls'   Mom's

2. ______________________________

3. ______________________________

Children write routinely for a range of tasks, purposes, and audiences. Children practice various conventions of standard English.

Benchmark Vocabulary

Name ______________________

DIRECTIONS Write sentences using the words below.

college downtown

Write in Response to Reading

DIRECTIONS Revisit the illustrations on pp. 1–15 of *Alexander, Who Used to Be Rich Last Sunday*. Do the illustrations help you to better understand Alexander as a character? Use examples from the text to support your opinion.

Children demonstrate contextual understanding of Benchmark Vocabulary. Children read text closely and use text evidence in their written answers.

Name ________________________

DIRECTIONS Look at the illustration on p. 11 of *Alexander, Who Used to Be Rich Last Sunday.* Using evidence from the text, write several sentences that explain what the illustration tells you about the characters Alexander, Anthony, and Nick.

Children analyze and respond to literary and informational text.

Name ______________________

Writing

DIRECTIONS Tell about how the illustrations in *Alexander, Who Used to Be Rich Last Sunday* help you understand what sort of character Alexander is. Use examples from the text to support your answer.

Conventions

Plural Possessives Circle the plural possessives. Then write two of your own sentences using plural possessives.

1. kittens' student's cousins' boys' dad's

2. ______________________

3. ______________________

Children write routinely for a range of tasks, purposes, and audiences. Children practice various conventions of standard English.

Name ______________________

DIRECTIONS Write sentences using the words below.

fined accident

Write in Response to Reading

DIRECTIONS Review the web you completed. Write about one way Alexander responded to losing or spending his money. Use examples from the text to support your answer.

Children demonstrate contextual understanding of Benchmark Vocabulary. Children read text closely and use text evidence in their written answers.

Name ______________________

Sleuth Work

I'll Trade You!

Samuel couldn't wait to show his mom and grandma the new skateboard he had just gotten from Ben. Ben couldn't wait to give his sister the new shawl he had just gotten from Samuel. Ben and Samuel were best friends!

Samuel's grandma had worked for weeks knitting the shawl. Ben had wondered for weeks what to get his sister for her birthday. Then one night Ben saw the shawl Samuel's grandma was knitting. He knew his sister would love it!

Samuel spent every day after school skateboarding with Ben. Samuel wished for his own skateboard. Ben knew how much Samuel would love having a skateboard. Suddenly a trade was born!

Trading one thing for another was a way of life. Samuel's mom and grandma remembered when people used something called money instead. Money paid for things they needed. Samuel and Ben were too young to remember that time.

Sometimes, Samuel's mother opened a secret drawer in her jewelry box. She let him hold the shiny coins and smooth dollar bills she had saved. Then they were put away for safekeeping.

Children read text closely to determine what the text says.

Name ___________________________

People no longer used money. They traded things instead. Samuel couldn't imagine life any other way. Samuel knew how to draw, so he always traded his drawings to get what he wanted. His family and Ben's family traded often. Samuel didn't understand why anyone might need money. Trading was so much easier!

Look for Clues
Underline details that support the fact that this story takes place in the future.

Ask Questions
On a separate sheet of paper, write a question you would ask Samuel and Ben about life without money.

Make Your Case
Underline the text that tells the most important idea the writer wants to share with readers about trading.

Make Your Case: Extend Your Ideas
Do you agree that trading is easier than using money? Write an opinion about this.

____

____

Children read text closely to determine what the text says.

Name ______________________________

Writing

DIRECTIONS Revisit p. 17 of *Alexander, Who Used to Be Rich Last Sunday*. Consider Alexander's actions in this scene. Then write a narrative sentence for each event on the page. Use specific words to describe the actions seen in the illustrations.

Conventions

Apostrophes Underline the contractions. Circle the possessive nouns.

1. can't don't isn't kids'

2. I've used the last bus pass!

3. I can't find the child's hat.

Children write routinely for a range of tasks, purposes, and audiences. Children practice various conventions of standard English.

Benchmark Vocabulary

Name ______________________________

DIRECTIONS Write sentences using the words below.

coins bargain savings

Write in Response to Reading

DIRECTIONS Think about how the characters in the story solved their problem. Then write a few sentences that tell how the girl earns money to help her family. Use examples from the text to support your answer.

Children demonstrate contextual understanding of Benchmark Vocabulary. Children read text closely and use text evidence in their written answers.

Name ____________________

DIRECTIONS Using evidence from the text, write sentences about the beginning, middle, and end of *A Chair for My Mother*. Use details from the text to support your answer.

Beginning:

Middle:

End:

Children analyze and respond to literary and informational text.

Writing

Name ______________________________

DIRECTIONS On a separate sheet of paper, write a new beginning to *A Chair for My Mother*. Start your new beginning at the time of the fire. Include vivid details to describe the fire. Revisit *A Chair for My Mother* to find details that show how the girl and her mother discovered the fire.

Conventions

Possessive Pronouns Write your own sentences using possessive pronouns.

1. ______________________________

2. ______________________________

3. ______________________________

Children write routinely for a range of tasks, purposes, and audiences. Children practice various conventions of standard English.

Name ______________________________

Benchmark Vocabulary

DIRECTIONS Write sentences using the words below.

spoiled charcoal

Write in Response to Reading

DIRECTIONS Revisit pp. 50–67 of *A Chair for My Mother*. Write several sentences about your opinion of the girl's character. Use details from the text to support your answer.

Children demonstrate contextual understanding of Benchmark Vocabulary. Children read text closely and use text evidence in their written answers.

Name ______________________________

DIRECTIONS Using evidence from the text, answer the following questions about pp. 50–67 of *A Chair for My Mother*.

1. Reread p. 53. What does this page tell you about the girl's character?

2. Reread the last paragraph on p. 55. Write several sentences about whether or not you think the girl's mother works hard. Use details from the text to support your answer.

Children analyze and respond to literary and informational text.

Name ____________________

Writing

DIRECTIONS Revisit the first half of *A Chair for My Mother*. Choose an event and write dialogue between the narrator and her mother about that event. Remember to use details to describe the characters' thoughts or feelings.

Conventions

Possessive Pronouns Circle the possessive pronouns in the sentences below. Then write your own sentence using a possessive pronoun.

1. This house is ours.

2. Is this your ruler?

3.

Children write routinely for a range of tasks, purposes, and audiences. Children practice various conventions of standard English.

Name ______________________

r-Controlled *ar, or, ore, oar*

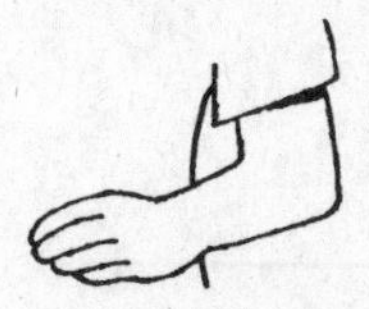

<u>ar</u>m

h<u>or</u>n

c<u>ore</u>

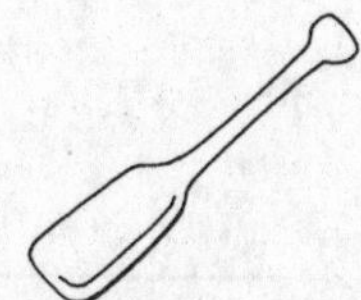

<u>oar</u>

Pick a word from the box to match each picture.
Write the word on the line.

artist	bark	garden	roar	score
store	stork	storm	start	short

1. 

____

2. 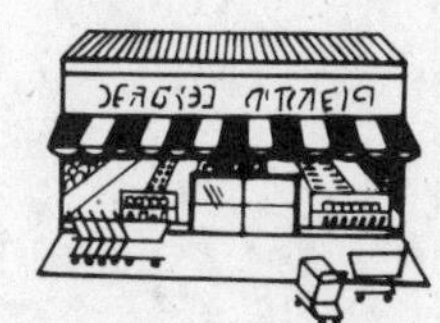

____

3. 

____

4. 

____

5. 

____

6. 

____

7. 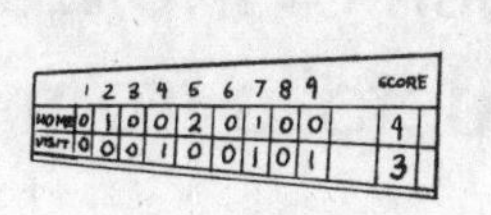

____

8. 

____

Pick a word that is the opposite of each word below.
Write the word on the line.

9. stop ______________________

10. tall ______________________

Children apply grade-level phonics and word analysis skills.

Benchmark Vocabulary

Name ______________________________

DIRECTIONS Write sentences using the words below.

exchanged boost

Write in Response to Reading

DIRECTIONS Revisit pp. 75–79 of *A Chair for My Mother*. Write several sentences about why the girl was not allowed to ride in the back of the truck while the chair was being delivered. Use details from the text to support your answer.

Children demonstrate contextual understanding of Benchmark Vocabulary. Children read text closely and use text evidence in their written answers.

Name ______________________

Writing

DIRECTIONS Write about the next item that the family will save up for. Include one detail that describes the item and one detail that describes the reason the family would want to save for the item. Revisit *A Chair for My Mother* to look for ideas about what the family might purchase.

Conventions

Simple Sentences Circle the simple sentences below. Then write your own simple sentence.

1. The sun was hot that day, so the pool felt cool. I had fun.
2. Although I couldn't ride in the truck, I was excited for the chair to be delivered. I was happy!
3. ______________________

Children write routinely for a range of tasks, purposes, and audiences. Children practice various conventions of standard English.

Name ______________________

Benchmark Vocabulary

DIRECTIONS Write a sentence using the word below.

rich

Write in Response to Reading

DIRECTIONS Write your thoughts about how the author structured the story—telling readers how it ends on the first page. Use details from the text to support your answer.

Children demonstrate contextual understanding of Benchmark Vocabulary. Children read text closely and use text evidence in their written answers.

Name ______________________________

DIRECTIONS Review the story sequence chart for *Alexander, Who Used to Be Rich Last Sunday*. Draw three pictures: one showing something that happened first, a second showing something that happened in the middle of the story, and a third picture showing something that happened last.

Children analyze and respond to literary and informational text.

Name ______________________

Writing

DIRECTIONS Write a new ending to *Alexander, Who Used to Be Rich Last Sunday.* Begin by choosing the characters that will be part of your ending. Then make sure that your ending follows the events of the beginning and middle of the story. Use adjectives to describe what happens.

Conventions

Expanding Simple Sentences Rewrite the sentences below by adding an adjective.

1. I found a penny on the sidewalk.

2. My family bought a chair.

3. He saw a spider.

Children write routinely for a range of tasks, purposes, and audiences. Children practice various conventions of standard English.

Benchmark Vocabulary

Name ______________________

DIRECTIONS Write sentences using the words below.

absolutely vanish

Write in Response to Reading

DIRECTIONS Revisit pp. 19–25 of *Alexander, Who Used to Be Rich Last Sunday*. Write an opinion about the way Alexander spent his money. Use details from the text to support your answer.

Children demonstrate contextual understanding of Benchmark Vocabulary. Children read text closely and use text evidence in their written answers.

Name ______________________

Reading Analysis

DIRECTIONS Reread pp. 19–25 of *Alexander, Who Used to Be Rich Last Sunday*. Think about how the main idea and key details help you to better understand the main character. Write several sentences that describe what type of character Alexander is. Use details from the text to support your answer.

Children analyze and respond to literary and informational text.

Name ______________________________

DIRECTIONS The book *Alexander, Who Used to Be Rich Last Sunday* does not use any dialogue. Write a dialogue between two of the characters during one of the events of the book. Make sure to use speaker tags to identify each character and to use quotation marks correctly. Revisit the text to look for ideas.

Expanding Simple Sentences Rewrite the sentences below using adverbs.

1. "I read my book."

2. She walked into the library.

3. The cat purred.

Children write routinely for a range of tasks, purposes, and audiences. Children practice various conventions of standard English.

Name ______________________________

Benchmark Vocabulary

DIRECTIONS Write a sentence using the word below.

positively

Write in Response to Reading

DIRECTIONS Revisit pp. 26–32 of *Alexander, Who Used to Be Rich Last Sunday.* Write an e-mail from Alexander's point of view to his parents, telling them what he learned. Use details from the text to support your answer.

Children demonstrate contextual understanding of Benchmark Vocabulary. Children read text closely and use text evidence in their written answers.

Name ______________________

Writing

DIRECTIONS Return to the dialogue you wrote in Lesson 8. Revise and edit your writing, looking for places to add or change words. Look for and correct errors in grammar, punctuation, and capitalization. Remember that adjectives and adverbs will help readers form clear and interesting pictures in their minds. Then copy your revised and edited work onto a fresh sheet of paper.

Conventions

Compound Subjects Write sentences using the compound subjects, "Felix and Max," "The teacher and her students," and "The dog and the cat."

1. ______________________

2. ______________________

3. ______________________

Children write routinely for a range of tasks, purposes, and audiences. Children practice various conventions of standard English.

Name ______________________

Benchmark Vocabulary

DIRECTIONS Write sentences using the words below.

tulips   block

Write in Response to Reading

DIRECTIONS Revisit *A Chair for My Mother.* Do you think the illustrations help you to imagine what it would be like if your own house burned down? Use details from the text to support your answer.

Children demonstrate contextual understanding of Benchmark Vocabulary. Children read text closely and use text evidence in their written answers.

Name ______________________

DIRECTIONS Using evidence from the text, answer the following question about *A Chair for My Mother.*

1. Reread pp. 62–63 of *A Chair for My Mother.* How does the illustration support the text on p. 63? Do you think the story would be the same without the illustrations? Use examples from the text to support your answer.

Children analyze and respond to literary and informational text.

Name ______________________________

Writing

DIRECTIONS Think back to the characters in *A Chair for My Mother.* Choose a character from the story, identify the main events, and create a Character Web to show how the character responds to those events.

Conventions

Using Verbs in Sentences Use the words below to complete each sentence.

sees walked played feeds

1. I ______________ to the park and ______________ frisbee.

2. She ______________ the ducks and ______________ them.

Children write routinely for a range of tasks, purposes, and audiences. Children practice various conventions of standard English.

Name ___________________________

r-Controlled *ar, or, ore, oar*

b**oar** c**ore** f**or**k be**ar**

Pick a word from the box to match each picture.
Write the word on the line.

shark	shore	bore	thorn	score
snore	roar	cart	porch	star

1.  ______________

2.  ______________

3. 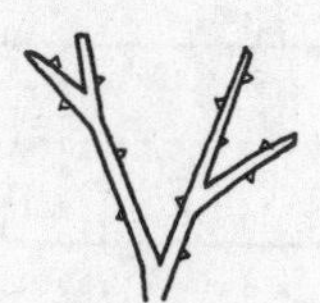 ______________

4. 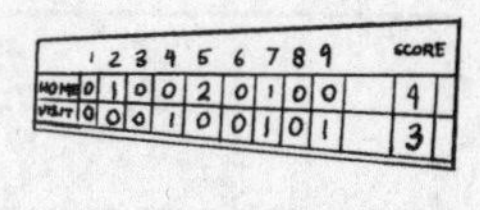 ______________

5.  ______________

6.  ______________

7.  ______________

8.  ______________

Pick a word that means the opposite of each word below.
Write the word on the line.

9. entertain ______________

10. not carry ______________

Children apply grade-level phonics and word analysis skills.

Name ______________________

Benchmark Vocabulary

DIRECTIONS Write sentences using the words below.

exchanged savings

Write in Response to Reading

DIRECTIONS Write a compare and contrast statement about the plots of *Alexander, Who Used to Be Rich Last Sunday* and *A Chair for My Mother.* Use details from both texts to support your answer.

Children demonstrate contextual understanding of Benchmark Vocabulary. Children read text closely and use text evidence in their written answers.

Name ______________________________

DIRECTIONS Revise your writing from Lesson 10. Add sequence words to your Character Web that expand on your characters' responses.

Conventions

Compound Sentences Combine the simple sentences below using *and* or *but.*

1. The rain fell. The thunder boomed.

2. I lost my tooth. It wasn't the first one I lost.

Children write routinely for a range of tasks, purposes, and audiences. Children practice various conventions of standard English.

Name ______________________________

Benchmark Vocabu

DIRECTIONS Write a sentence using the word below.

rich

Write in Response to Reading

DIRECTIONS Write an opinion about the character you think has the better approach to money—Alexander or the girl. Use details from the texts to support your opinion.

Children demonstrate contextual understanding of Benchmark Vocabulary. Children read text closely and use text evidence in their written answers.

Name ______________________________

DIRECTIONS Review the T-Chart you created that lists Alexander's point of view and the girl's point of view in *Alexander, Who Used to Be Rich Last Sunday* and *A Chair for My Mother.* Using evidence from the text, write a comparison statement about how these two characters' points of view are similar or different. Use evidence from each text to support your answer.

Children analyze and respond to literary and informational text.

Name ______________________

Writing

DIRECTIONS Choose a character from one of the texts to write a narrative about. Your narrative should tell about the choices that character makes in the story. Use details from the text to support your answer.

Conventions

Compound Sentences Write compound sentences that use the word *and*.

1.

2.

Children write routinely for a range of tasks, purposes, and audiences. Children practice various conventions of standard English.

Name ______________________

Benchmark Vocabulary

DIRECTIONS Write sentences using the words below.

save bargain

Write in Response to Reading

DIRECTIONS Write several sentences about which character you like more–Alexander or the girl. What do the pictures tell you about the character you prefer? Use details from both texts to support your answer.

Children demonstrate contextual understanding of Benchmark Vocabulary. Children read text closely and use text evidence in their written answers.

Name ______________________________

Sleuth Work

More Than Cash Dispensers

Have you ever visited an ATM? Did you stare in wonder when, like magic, money came out of the machine? Several decades ago banking wasn't so convenient.

People use banks to safely keep and save money. Then, when they need to spend it, they withdraw the money. That's hard to do if your bank isn't nearby. It's even harder to do if your bank is closed. So how do you get cash when you need it?

In the early 1970s, the first ATM, or automated teller machine, was introduced. Using a plastic bank card and a PIN, or personal identification number, people could access their bank accounts. They could do this at any time of day or night or even when the bank was closed. They could withdraw money, and they could deposit money and checks. ATMs started springing up everywhere, making it easy for people to withdraw money from their bank accounts.

Banks are adding new ATM services every year. For example, people can now deposit checks without using an envelope. That's because ATMs scan, or read, checks. Another improvement is talking ATMs. These machines have audio, so people that cannot see well or at all can access their bank accounts by listening to instructions.

Children read text closely to determine what the text says.

Name ______________________________

ATMs keep improving. Some ATMs now have video screens. A banker uses the video screen to talk with the person using the ATM. Other banks are even testing ways mobile phones can be used at ATMs. Just imagine what ATMs will be able to do next!

Look for Clues
Underline one piece of evidence from the text that tells how modern ATMs are different from ATMs from the early 1970s.

Ask Questions
Write a question you have about ATMs.

____

Make Your Case
Underline the most convincing statement the writer makes to support the idea that ATMs are more than just cash dispensers.

Make Your Case: Extend Your Ideas
Write why you agree or disagree that ATMs are more than cash dispensers.

____

Children read text closely to determine what the text says.

Name ______________________________

Writing

DIRECTIONS Reread the narrative writing you did in Lesson 12. Revise your narrative to make it stronger and more descriptive. Remember to include graphics or pictures in your display.

Conventions

Compound Sentences Write compound sentences that use the word *but*.

1.

2.

Children write routinely for a range of tasks, purposes, and audiences. Children practice various conventions of standard English.

Name ________________________

Contractions

Read the contractions in the box.
Pick the contraction that is formed from each pair of words.
Write the contraction on the line.

It is happy.
It's happy.

can't	haven't	he's	I'm	she's	they'll	we'll	who's

1. have + not ____________

2. I + am ____________

3. can + not ____________

4. they + will ____________

5. who + is ____________

6. we + will ____________

Circle the contraction in each sentence.

7. He's her little brother.
8. She's his big sister.
9. Lisa hasn't eaten lunch yet.
10. Steven can't hear who's knocking!

Children apply grade-level phonics and word analysis skills.

Name ______________________

Benchmark Vocabulary

DIRECTIONS Write a sentence using the word below.

spending

Write in Response to Reading

DIRECTIONS Reread pp. 18–19 of *Money Matters!* Write several sentences about the main purpose of these pages. Use examples from the text to support your answer.

Children demonstrate contextual understanding of Benchmark Vocabulary. Children read text closely and use text evidence in their written answers.

Name ______________________

Writing

DIRECTIONS Write an opinion about whether or not the author of *Money Matters!* achieved her purpose of informing people about money and how it matters to people. Give reasons from the text to support your opinion.

Conventions

Commas in a Series Write two new sentences, each using commas in a series, on the lines below.

1.

2.

Children write routinely for a range of tasks, purposes, and audiences. Children practice various conventions of standard English.

Name ____________________

Benchmark Vocabulary

DIRECTIONS Write sentences using the words below.

earn choices

Write in Response to Reading

DIRECTIONS Reread p. 6 of *Money Matters!* When do you think it is appropriate to make a trade? Use the text to support your answer.

Children demonstrate contextual understanding of Benchmark Vocabulary. Children read text closely and use text evidence in their written answers.

Name ______________________

DIRECTIONS Using evidence from the text, answer the following questions about pp. 4–9 of *Money Matters!*

1. Reread the first paragraph on p. 6 of *Money Matters!* Write several sentences about how the information on that page relates to the main topic. Use examples from the text to support your answer.

2. Reread p. 9 of *Money Matters!* What items have been used as currency in the past?

3. Which item of currency most surprises you?

Children analyze and respond to literary and informational text.

Name ______________________________

Writing

DIRECTIONS Write a paragraph about why you think it is important to make good decisions. Remember to use the answers to your three questions, as well as the ideas you discussed with your partner.

Conventions

Commas in Compound Sentences Write two of your own compound sentences using commas.

1.

2.

Children write routinely for a range of tasks, purposes, and audiences. Children practice various conventions of standard English.

Name ______________________

Benchmark Vocabulary

DIRECTIONS Write sentences using the words below.

agree   valuable   refuse

Write in Response to Reading

DIRECTIONS Reread p. 13 of *Money Matters!* What is a gold rush? How do you know? Use examples from the text to support your answer.

Children demonstrate contextual understanding of Benchmark Vocabulary. Children read text closely and use text evidence in their written answers.

Name ______________________

Reading Analysis

DIRECTIONS Using evidence from the text, answer the following questions about pp. 10–15 of *Money Matters!*

1. Reread pp. 12–13. How do the text features on these pages help you locate key facts?

2. Reread pp. 14–15. How do the text features on these pages help you locate key facts?

3. What is counterfeit money? Use examples from the text to support your answer.

Children analyze and respond to literary and informational text.

Name ______________________

DIRECTIONS Write an opinion about the section of text you think is most helpful for your life. Remember to state your opinion clearly, include reasons to support your opinion, and to include at least one compound sentence that uses a comma.

Commas in Compound Sentences Write two of your own compound sentences using commas.

1. ______________________

2. ______________________

Children write routinely for a range of tasks, purposes, and audiences. Children practice various conventions of standard English.

Name ______________________________

Benchmark Vocabulary

DIRECTIONS Write sentences using the words below.

sold borrow bought

Write in Response to Reading

DIRECTIONS Reread pp. 16–17 of *Money Matters!* Why are banks a safe place to store money? Use examples from the text to support your answer.

Children demonstrate contextual understanding of Benchmark Vocabulary. Children read text closely and use text evidence in their written answers.

Name ____________________

DIRECTIONS Using evidence from the text, answer the following questions about pp. 16–19 of *Money Matters!*

1. Reread p. 17. What are debit and credit cards normally used for?

2. Reread pp. 18–19. What is a credit card?

3. How is a credit card different from cash?

4. Why is it important to track how much you spend if you're using a credit card?

Children analyze and respond to literary and informational text.

Name ______________________________

Writing

DIRECTIONS Write an opinion about whether you would use a debit or a credit card if you could. Remember to support your opinion with reasons. Use examples from the text to support your answer.

____

____

____

Conventions

Commas in Dates Add a comma to the dates below.

1. February 20 1990

____

2. December 21 1986

____

3. August 10 2005

____

Children write routinely for a range of tasks, purposes, and audiences. Children practice various conventions of standard English.

Benchmark Vocabulary

Name ______________________________

DIRECTIONS Write sentences using the words below.

services measures useful

Write in Response to Reading

DIRECTIONS Reread pp. 24–25 of *Money Matters!* What text features help you to understand what an entrepreneur is? Use examples from the text to support your answer.

Children demonstrate contextual understanding of Benchmark Vocabulary. Children read text closely and use text evidence in their written answers.

Name ______________________

DIRECTIONS Write a paragraph that tells about two questions you asked that were answered on pp. 22–25 of *Money Matters!*. Use evidence from the text. What text features helped you answer these questions?

Children analyze and respond to literary and informational text.

Name ____________________

DIRECTIONS Revisit a section of *Money Matters!* and write a sentence about its purpose. Include a description about the section's text features and the information it provides to readers. Then include an opinion about whether the text features helped support the author's purpose.

Commas and Adjectives Write two sentences using the adjective pairs below. Remember to use commas.

1. fuzzy pink **2.** tiny green

1.

2.

Children write routinely for a range of tasks, purposes, and audiences. Children practice various conventions of standard English.

Name ______________________________

r-Controlled *er, ir, ur*

f**<u>er</u>**n

b**<u>ir</u>**d

s**<u>ur</u>**f

Read the words. **Circle** the correct word for each picture.

1.

turtle torn

2.

short shirt

3.

herd hard

4.

nose nurse

Look at the first word. **Circle** the word in the sentence that has the same vowel sound as the first word.

her	**5.** I live around the corner from Amy.
burn	**6.** My mom puts her keys in her purse.
dirt	**7.** Liam was the first in line for lunch.
perch	**8.** We like to watch monster movies.

Children apply grade-level phonics and word analysis skills.

Benchmark Vocabulary

Name ______________________

DIRECTIONS Write sentences using the words below.

skills chores

Write in Response to Reading

DIRECTIONS Reread pp. 28–29 of *Money Matters!* Why do you think it's important to budget? Use examples from the text to support your answer.

Children demonstrate contextual understanding of Benchmark Vocabulary. Children read text closely and use text evidence in their written answers.

Name ______________________________ Writing

DIRECTIONS Write an opinion about what you think is more valuable – things or experiences? Use conjunctions to connect your reasons and points. Use examples from the text to support your answer.

Conventions

Commas Circle any sentence that uses commas correctly. Cross out any sentence that does not use commas correctly.

1. The tree branch fell and it landed, on my face.
2. I like credit cards because they're tiny, reliable, and secure.
3. Money can't buy you happiness, It can't help you live forever either.

Children write routinely for a range of tasks, purposes, and audiences. Children practice various conventions of standard English.

Benchmark Vocabulary

Name ______________________________

DIRECTIONS Write sentences using the words below.

doubt   compassionate

Write in Response to Reading

DIRECTIONS Write two questions you would want to ask Alex from the story *I Wanna Iguana*. Revisit the text to help you.

Children demonstrate contextual understanding of Benchmark Vocabulary. Children read text closely and use text evidence in their written answers.

Name ________________________________

DIRECTIONS Reread pp. 84–85 of *I Wanna Iguana*. Think about questions you find yourself asking as you read. Write your questions down, and then write the answers to your questions.

Children analyze and respond to literary and informational text.

Writing

Name ______________________

DIRECTIONS Revisit the opinion paragraph you wrote in Lesson 6. Revise your paragraph by adding additional reasons that support your opinion. Then add linking words or phrases to further strengthen your paragraph.

Conventions

Commas in Letters How would you start a letter to a friend? Write your greeting on the lines below. Then write a short letter of your own to a friend.

Greeting: ______________________

Children write routinely for a range of tasks, purposes, and audiences. Children practice various conventions of standard English.

Name ______________________________

Benchmark Vocabulary

DIRECTIONS Write sentences using the words below.

mention concerned

Write in Response to Reading

DIRECTIONS Many stories include dialogue, but *I Wanna Iguana* is told through a series of letters. Do you think the story would be better if it had dialogue?

Children demonstrate contextual understanding of Benchmark Vocabulary. Children read text closely and use text evidence in their written answers.

Name ______________________________

Another Movie Night to Remember

For weeks, I had seen a big, red circle on the calendar. It was my parents' anniversary. I got the sense this was an important day, and I wanted to do something to celebrate . . . but what?

Mom had once told us that Dad asked her to marry him after taking her out for pizza and a romantic movie. We decided to have a movie night that Mom and Dad would never forget.

We bought the ingredients to make Mom's favorite pizza. My older sister Bethany found out what movie they had seen, and we rented it for the night. But everything started to go wrong.

First, the pizza slid off the pan and onto the floor as I carried it to the table. Next, Bethany burned the popcorn, so the whole house smelled awful. Then we discovered that the DVD wouldn't play. Bethany and I were upset, but Dad chuckled as he opened a window to air out the house. He took us out to dinner, to the same restaurant where he and Mom had eaten that special night. Over pizza, we heard the story of how Mom and Dad met. It was better than the best romantic movie—even without popcorn!

Children read text closely to determine what the text says.

Name ________________________________

Look for Clues

Underline details that support the idea that Mom and Dad were not upset about the problems that happened with the surprise.

Ask Questions

On a separate piece of paper, write a question that you would ask someone who is celebrating a special day.

Ask Questions: Extend Your Ideas

What questions would you ask the girls who planned the event?

____

____

Make Your Case

Write three words or phrases that describe the narrator's feelings. Then, on a separate piece of paper, write a new version of the story, using your own words.

____

____

Make Your Case: Extend Your Ideas

Do you think it was smart for the girls to plan a surprise for their parents? On a separate piece of paper, write an opinion about this.

Children read text closely to determine what the text says.

Writing

Name ______________________

DIRECTIONS Choose a letter from Mom on pp. 81–87 in *I Wanna Iguana*. Then, on a separate sheet of paper, rewrite one of Alex's responses to that letter. Give different reasons to support the opinion you express in the letter. Make sure to list facts or reasons in your letter. Choose your words carefully to persuade Alex's mom to accept your opinion. Remember to use commas correctly in both the greeting and closing of your letter.

Conventions

Commas in Letters How would you finish a letter to a friend? Write your closing on the lines below. Remember to use commas correctly.

Children write routinely for a range of tasks, purposes, and audiences. Children practice various conventions of standard English.

Name ______________________________

Benchmark Vocabulary

DIRECTIONS Write a sentence using the word below.

exactly

Write in Response to Reading

DIRECTIONS Reread pp. 91–92 of *I Wanna Iguana.* What do you know about Alex's father? Do you think he is more like his wife or Alex? Write a few sentences that explain your opinion. Use details from the text to support your opinion.

Children demonstrate contextual understanding of Benchmark Vocabulary. Children read text closely and use text evidence in their written answers.

Name ______________________

Reread pp. 88–95 of *I Wanna Iguana.* Choose a character from the text and list some of his or her traits on the lines below. Then write several sentences about the character you chose. Why do you like him or her? Use examples from the text to support your answer.

Character: ______________________

Trait 1: ______________________

Trait 2: ______________________

Trait 3: ______________________

Why?: ______________________

____

____

____

____

Children analyze and respond to literary and informational text.

Name ______________________________

Writing

DIRECTIONS Review pages 88–95 in *I Wanna Iguana.* Look at the details the author uses to describe Alex's character. On a separate piece of paper, write a letter to Alex's mom as if you were a friend of Alex. Tell Alex's mom whether you think he should have the iguana or not. Make sure to give reasons that support your opinion.

Conventions

Commas in Letters Write the greetings below correctly.

1. Dear Uncle Mike

2. Dear, Mom

Children write routinely for a range of tasks, purposes, and audiences. Children practice various conventions of standard English.

Name ______________________________

Benchmark Vocabulary

DIRECTIONS Write sentences using the words below.

responsible financial

Write in Response to Reading

DIRECTIONS Write a few sentences to answer this question: Do you think Alex will take care of the iguana and be able to keep it? Use details from the text to support your answer.

Children demonstrate contextual understanding of Benchmark Vocabulary. Children read text closely and use text evidence in their written answers.

Name ______________________________

DIRECTIONS Using evidence from the text, answer the following questions about pp. 84–85 of *I Wanna Iguana.*

1. Reread p. 84. Is more than one point of view expressed on this page?

2. How do the text features on these pages help you figure out point of view?

3. Reread pp. 84–85. How is Alex's point of view different from his mom's?

Children analyze and respond to literary and informational text.

Name ______________________________

Writing

DIRECTIONS Think about what you have read in *I Wanna Iguana.* Decide whether you agree with Alex or his mom's point of view about having an iguana as a pet. Use details and reasons from the text to support your opinion.

Conventions

Use Commas Circle the closing that is correct. Then write your own short letter on the lines below.

1. Sincerely, Mackenzie   Sincerely Mackenzie

2.

Children write routinely for a range of tasks, purposes, and audiences. Children practice various conventions of standard English.

Name ______________________________

r-Controlled *er, ir, ur*

f**er**n b**ir**d s**ur**f

Read the words. **Write** the word for each picture.

1.

rocks dirt

____

2.

burn turn

____

3.

steer stir

____

4.

plate dinner

____

Look at the first word. **Circle** the word in the sentence that has the same vowel sound as the first word.

nurse **5.** The man at the store found my mother's purse and returned it to her.

squirt **6.** I was playing tag on the playground when my shirt ripped.

hamster **7.** My dog likes to sit under the table.

birthday **8.** Yesterday was the first time I ate a banana split!

Children apply grade-level phonics and word analysis skills.

Benchmark Vocabulary

Name ______________________________

DIRECTIONS Write sentences using the words below.

chores allowance

Write in Response to Reading

DIRECTIONS Reread p. 93 of *I Wanna Iguana* and pp. 26–27 of *Money Matters!* What do these two sections have in common? Use details from both texts to support your answer.

Children demonstrate contextual understanding of Benchmark Vocabulary. Children read text closely and use text evidence in their written answers.

Name ______________________

Writing

DIRECTIONS Reread the text on pp. 26–27 of *Money Matters!* and p. 93 of *I Wanna Iguana.* Write a paragraph about how you would spend your money. Use examples and details from the text to support your opinion.

Conventions

Simple Sentences Complete each sentence below to include the missing subject or predicate.

1. ______________________ wrote a letter to his mom.

2. The family ______________________.

Children write routinely for a range of tasks, purposes, and audiences. Children practice various conventions of standard English.

Name ______________________________

Benchmark Vocabulary

DIRECTIONS Write a sentence using the word below.

need

Write in Response to Reading

DIRECTIONS Think back to the two texts—*I Wanna Iguana* and *Money Matters!* Which text do you think gets its message across more clearly? Use details from the text to support your opinion.

Children demonstrate contextual understanding of Benchmark Vocabulary. Children read text closely and use text evidence in their written answers.

Name ______________________

DIRECTIONS Think back to the main topic and author's message in *I Wanna Iguana* and *Money Matters!* Write several sentences that compare and contrast the main topic of each book. Remember to include details from both texts to support your answer.

I Wanna Iguana:

Money Matters!:

Children analyze and respond to literary and informational text.

Writing

Name ____________________

DIRECTIONS Revise your opinion piece about using your own money wisely. Expand your writing using reasons and evidence from the text and your own opinions about handling money. Remember that you can strengthen your message by including details and examples.

Conventions

Expanding Simple Sentences Add or change words to expand the simple sentences below.

1. My family needs a budget.

2. Do you have a lot of coins?

Children write routinely for a range of tasks, purposes, and audiences. Children practice various conventions of standard English.

Name ______________________

Plurals

Write the word for each picture. **Use** the words in the box to help you.
Add *-s*, *-es*, change the ***y*** to ***i*** and add ***-es***, or change the ***f*** to ***v*** and add ***-es***.

bunny	bush	calf	fork	fox
house	leaf	candy	shelf	spoon

1. 

2. 

3. 

4. 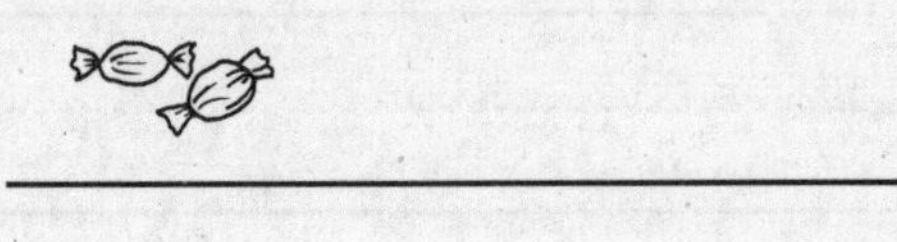

5. 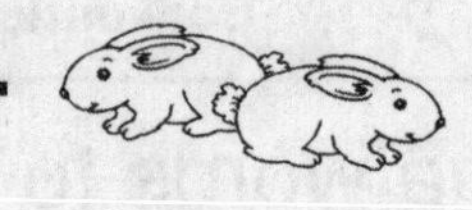

6. 

7. 

8. 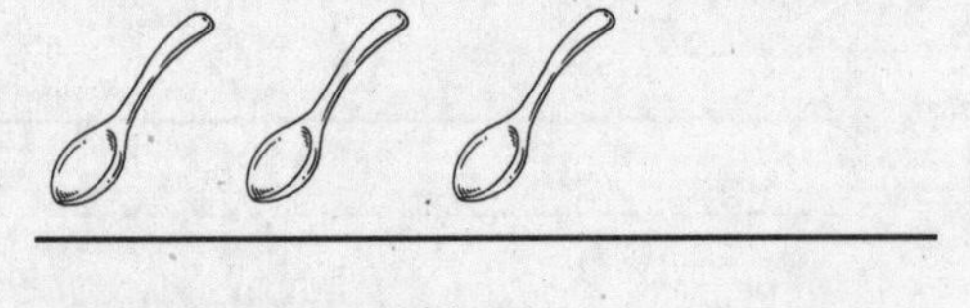

9. 

10.

Children apply grade-level phonics and word analysis skills.

Benchmark Vocabulary

Name ______________________________

DIRECTIONS Write sentences using the words below.

unusual   energy

Write in Response to Reading

DIRECTIONS Reread pp. 1–9 of *Theodore Roosevelt: The Adventurous President.* Think about the subheadings found throughout the section. What was Teddy Roosevelt like as a child? What subheading helps you to answer this question?

Children demonstrate contextual understanding of Benchmark Vocabulary. Children read text closely and use text evidence in their written answers.

Name ______________________

Writing

DIRECTIONS Think about Chapters 1 and 2 of *Theodore Roosevelt: The Adventurous President*. Write a few sentences about something you have learned and explain how it applies to your life.

Conventions

Capitalizing Geographic Names Rewrite the correct geographical names on the lines below. Then write your own sentence using a capitalized geographical name correctly.

1. I live in the city of chicago. ______________

2. My older sister traveled to shanghai with her friends. ______________

3. ______________

Children write routinely for a range of tasks, purposes, and audiences. Children practice various conventions of standard English.

Benchmark Vocabulary

Name ______________________________

DIRECTIONS Write sentences using the words below.

honor politics

Write in Response to Reading

DIRECTIONS Think about Chapters 3, 4, and 5 of *Theodore Roosevelt: The Adventurous President*. Write several sentences about your opinion of Theodore Roosevelt so far. Use details from the text to support your answer.

Children demonstrate contextual understanding of Benchmark Vocabulary. Children read text closely and use text evidence in their written answers.

Name ______________________________

DIRECTIONS Using evidence from *Theodore Roosevelt: The Adventurous President,* follow the directions below.

1. Think back to today's reading. Write one unanswered question that you asked while reading.

2. Tell how you might find the answer to that question.

3. Write one question that you asked that was answered by the text.

4. Write the answer to that question.

Children analyze and respond to literary and informational text.

Writing

Name ______________________________

DIRECTIONS Revisit the first few chapters of *Theodore Roosevelt: The Adventurous President*. Write down two ways that Teddy Roosevelt was building ideas for his family, New York City, and his country. Use details from the text to support your answer.

Conventions

Capitalizing Geographic Names Rewrite the correct states and regions on the lines below. Then write your own sentence using a capitalized geographical name correctly.

1. My grandma moved to richmond. ______________

2. We studied the state of new york last week.

____

3. ______________

Children write routinely for a range of tasks, purposes, and audiences. Children practice various conventions of standard English.

Name ______________________

Benchmark Vocabulary

DIRECTIONS Write sentences using the words below.

popular strike

Write in Response to Reading

DIRECTIONS Revisit Chapter 6 of *Theodore Roosevelt: The Adventurous President*. Choose a photo and write one or two sentences about what the photo tells you. Use details to support your answer.

Children demonstrate contextual understanding of Benchmark Vocabulary. Children read text closely and use text evidence in their written answers.

Name ______________________________

Gregor Mendel

Gregor Mendel always loved nature. He grew up on a farm. He walked through the countryside every day. He loved to look at plants and animals along the way. He noticed the ways plants are alike and different. Later, Mendel became a teacher and scientist.

One day Mendel took a long walk. He saw a flower that was different from others of the same kind. It made him wonder. What caused such differences? He began to grow pea plants as part of an experiment. In seven years, he grew thousands of plants! He kept track of different traits in plants. He noticed the color of the flowers and pea pods. He measured the height of the plants.

He noticed the shape of their pods and leaves. He saw that there was a pattern. "Parent" plants passed traits to "daughter" plants in certain ways. Mendel's studies helped him discover rules about how traits are passed on. This was the beginning of a branch of science called genetics.

Genetics has helped scientists and doctors understand more about all living things. Scientists can fight disease and grow healthier food. Next time you are curious about something, explore it! Who knows? You, like Gregor Mendel, could change the world.

Children read text closely to determine what the text says.

Name ______________________

Sleuth Work

Look for Clues

Underline details that tell what made Mendel a good scientist.

Ask Questions

Write a question that was not answered about Mendel in the text.

____

Ask Questions: Extend Your Ideas

Write a question that a reporter might ask Mendel about his research. Use the text to formulate your question. Then underline the text that Mendel would use to answer the question.

____

Make Your Case

Circle three facts in the text that tell about Mendel's life. Then write one fact you would like to know about him.

____

Children read text closely to determine what the text says.

Name ______________________

Writing

DIRECTIONS Create an idea for a new text feature to add to *Theodore Roosevelt: The Adventurous President*. What is it? Where will it go? What information will it tell? Explain how the text feature you create will support the text.

Conventions

Capitalizing Geographic Names Rewrite the correct country names on the lines below. Then write your own sentence using a capitalized geographical name correctly.

1. Tanya is from mexico. ______________

2. Beijing is a major city in china. ______________

3. ______________________________

Children write routinely for a range of tasks, purposes, and audiences. Children practice various conventions of standard English.

Name ______________________

Benchmark Vocabulary

DIRECTIONS Write sentences using the words below.

experts extinct

Write in Response to Reading

DIRECTIONS Revisit Chapters 7–8 of *Theodore Roosevelt: The Adventurous President*. Write a few sentences that tell about how Teddy and his family were affected by the three wars that occurred during his lifetime. Use details from the text to support your answer.

Children demonstrate contextual understanding of Benchmark Vocabulary. Children read text closely and use text evidence in their written answers.

Name ________________________________

DIRECTIONS Using evidence from the text, answer the following questions about Chapters 1–8 of *Theodore Roosevelt: The Adventurous President*.

1. List three major historical events that occurred during Teddy Roosevelt's lifetime:

2. Pick one of the historical events above and tell how it affected Teddy Roosevelt's life.

3. Revisit pp. 10–12. Why does Teddy decide to go into politics? Use details to support your answer.

Children analyze and respond to literary and informational text.

Name ____________________

Writing

DIRECTIONS Look through *Theodore Roosevelt: The Adventurous President*. Write about an event that shows Teddy Roosevelt was a creator of ideas or made contributions to the country. Use details from the text to support your answer.

Conventions

Capitalizing Geographic Names Correctly capitalize the continents in the sentences below. Then write your own sentence using a capitalized geographical name correctly.

1. Teddy often went hunting in africa. ____________

2. I cannot wait to travel to asia next summer! ____________

3. ____________________

Children write routinely for a range of tasks, purposes, and audiences. Children practice various conventions of standard English.

Benchmark Vocabulary

Name ___________________________

DIRECTIONS Write sentences using the words below.

grateful conservation

Write in Response to Reading

DIRECTIONS Write three questions that you would ask Teddy Roosevelt or Charles Markis, who was interviewed about Roosevelt.

Children demonstrate contextual understanding of Benchmark Vocabulary. Children read text closely and use text evidence in their written answers.

Name ______________________________

DIRECTIONS Using evidence from the text, answer the following questions about pp. 42–44 of *Theodore Roosevelt: The Adventurous President.*

1. List three words that helped you find key details about Teddy Roosevelt in the interview.

2. How many acres of land did Teddy Roosevelt set aside during his presidency?

3. Have other presidents followed Teddy's example?

4. Write several sentences about why you think it's important to protect wilderness areas. Use details from the text to support your answer.

Children analyze and respond to literary and informational text.

Name ____________________

Writing

DIRECTIONS Pick a topic that you would like to know more about. Then list three questions you would like to research about that topic, and tell why you are interested in those questions.

Conventions

Proper Nouns Capitalize the national parks in the sentences below. Then write your own sentence using a capitalized geographical name correctly.

1. We hiked in yellowstone. ____________________

2. After reading about Teddy Roosevelt, I traveled to sagamore hill. ____________________

3. ____________________

Children write routinely for a range of tasks, purposes, and audiences. Children practice various conventions of standard English.

Name ______________________________

Phonics

Long *a* Spelled *a, ai, ay*

Read each sentence.

Write the word with the **long *a*** sound on the line below.

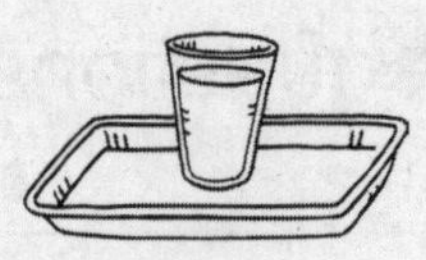

tail **tray**

1. The ducklings play in the water. ______________

2. The baby ducks do not see the cat. ______________

3. It is waiting in the grass. ______________

4. The big ducks are not afraid of the cat. ______________

5. The cat runs away as fast as it can. ______________

6. We bought a new table. ______________

Children apply grade-level phonics and word analysis skills.

Benchmark Vocabulary

Name ______________________________

DIRECTIONS Write sentences using the words below.

preserve proverb

Write in Response to Reading

DIRECTIONS Reread the sidebars on pp. 8, 19, 30–31, 37, and 40 in *Theodore Roosevelt: The Adventurous President*. Then write a sentence or two that tells about the sidebar you find most interesting. Use details from the text to support your answer.

Children demonstrate contextual understanding of Benchmark Vocabulary. Children read text closely and use text evidence in their written answers.

Name ______________________________

Writing

DIRECTIONS Choose a topic from the brainstorm and create a quotation that Roosevelt would have said or believed. Then explain how the quotation fits with his actions.

Conventions

Adjectives Circle the adjectives in the sentences below. Then write 5 adjectives that describe your bedroom.

1. Our family hiked the rugged trail. We often had to stop to wait for my little sister to catch up. She constantly fell behind us. It really was a long, hot hike.

2.

Children write routinely for a range of tasks, purposes, and audiences. Children practice various conventions of standard English.

Benchmark Vocabulary

Name ___________________________

DIRECTIONS Write a sentence using the word below.

weary

Write in Response to Reading

DIRECTIONS Think about the details the poet included about Abraham Lincoln's life. Then look at the illustration. Why do you think the poet chose to focus on Lincoln's childhood?

Children demonstrate contextual understanding of Benchmark Vocabulary. Children read text closely and use text evidence in their written answers.

Name ______________________________

DIRECTIONS Make a list of the rhyming words you found in the second, third, and fourth stanzas in "Lincoln" on pp. 166–167.

Stanza Two:

Stanza Three:

Stanza Four:

Children analyze and respond to literary and informational text.

Name ________________________

DIRECTIONS Write three questions that you might want to research about Abraham Lincoln's life. Research one of the questions. Then write a paragraph that provides the answer to that question.

Adverbs Write your own sentences using adverbs that describe *how, when,* and *where.*

1.

2.

3.

Children write routinely for a range of tasks, purposes, and audiences. Children practice various conventions of standard English.

Name ______________________

Benchmark Vocabulary

DIRECTIONS Write sentences using the words below.

rights strenuous swarmed

Write in Response to Reading

DIRECTIONS Reread pp. 103–109 of *Marching with Aunt Susan.* Based on what you have read so far, write your opinion of Bessie and her brothers. Use details from the text to support your answer.

Children demonstrate contextual understanding of Benchmark Vocabulary. Children read text closely and use text evidence in their written answers.

Name ______________________________

DIRECTIONS Reread pp. 106–109 of *Marching with Aunt Susan.* Write one question that you asked yourself while you read these pages. Then write the answer to that question. Use details from the text to support your answer.

Children analyze and respond to literary and informational text.

Name ______________________________

Writing

DIRECTIONS Identify the time period of *Marching with Aunt Susan*. Write three questions about that time period. Then list three sources you might use to find more information about the time period.

Conventions

Adverbs Write your own sentences using adverbs.

1.

2.

3.

Children write routinely for a range of tasks, purposes, and audiences. Children practice various conventions of standard English.

Name ________________________________

Benchmark Vocabulary

DIRECTIONS Write sentences using the words below.

mount balance wobbling

Write in Response to Reading

DIRECTIONS Reread pp. 120–131 of *Marching with Aunt Susan.* Name one part of the story that is probably made up. Then name one part of the story that is probably true. Use examples from the text to support your answer.

Children demonstrate contextual understanding of Benchmark Vocabulary. Children read text closely and use text evidence in their written answers.

Name ______________________

Writing

DIRECTIONS Research Susan B. Anthony. Then write a paragraph that tells your opinion of Susan B. Anthony and what she did in her life. Use examples from your research and the text to support your answer.

Conventions

Adjectives and Adverbs Write sentences that use adjectives and adverbs. Circle the adjectives and underline the adverbs.

1.

2.

3.

Children write routinely for a range of tasks, purposes, and audiences. Children practice various conventions of standard English.

Name ______________________________

Benchmark Vocabulary

DIRECTIONS Write sentences using the words below.

avid portrait

Write in Response to Reading

DIRECTIONS Reread pp. 132–135 of *Marching with Aunt Susan*. Do you think the author did a good job connecting Bessie's life with Susan B. Anthony? Use details from the text to support your answer.

Children demonstrate contextual understanding of Benchmark Vocabulary. Children read text closely and use text evidence in their written answers.

Name ______________________

DIRECTIONS Review the Story Sequence graphic organizer that tells the sequence of the historical events in *Marching with Aunt Susan*. What historical event occurred after the election? Write several sentences that tell about that event.

Children analyze and respond to literary and informational text.

Name ______________________________

DIRECTIONS Review the Author's Note in *Marching with Aunt Susan*. Write a paragraph that explains a connection between the characters or events in the story, and something mentioned in the Author's Note. Use facts from both the note and the story to explain the connection. Include a concluding sentence that restates the connection.

Adjectives and Adverbs Match the adjective or adverb with the word it describes. Then write your own sentence using an adjective or an adverb.

1. loud — a. whistled
2. softly — b. music
3. carefully — c. painted
4. ______________________________

Children write routinely for a range of tasks, purposes, and audiences. Children practice various conventions of standard English.

Name ______________________________

Phonics

Long *e* Spelled *e, ee, ea, y*

These bees only fly past words with the long ***e*** sound.
Circle each word with the **long *e*** sound.
Draw a line to show the path from the bees to the tree.

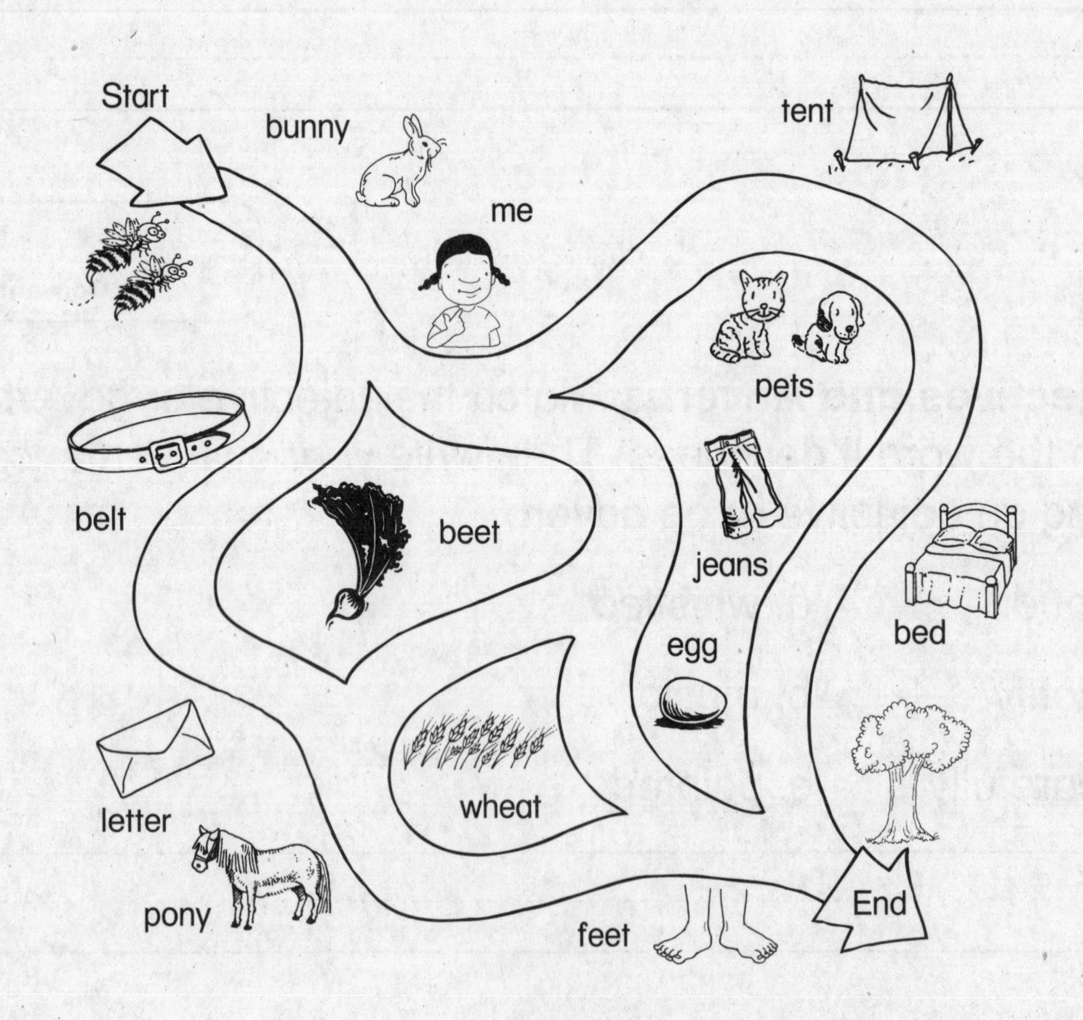

Children apply grade-level phonics and word analysis skills.

Name ______________________________

Benchmark Vocabulary

DIRECTIONS Write sentences using the words below.

rights avid

Write in Response to Reading

DIRECTIONS Think about some of the differences in the way boys and girls are thought of in this story. How have some points of view about boys and girls **not** changed since the time period of the story? Use examples to support your answer.

Children demonstrate contextual understanding of Benchmark Vocabulary. Children read text closely and use text evidence in their written answers.

Name ______________________

Writing

DIRECTIONS Select someone from either text other than Teddy Roosevelt or Susan B. Anthony to research. Research that person with other classmates who chose the same person. Make a list of the resources you used for research and take notes. Then make a list of the facts you found, putting them in a logical order.

Conventions

Expand Sentences with Adjectives Rewrite the sentences on the lines below, adding adjectives.

1. The cat chased the dog.

2. We spent the day at the beach.

Children write routinely for a range of tasks, purposes, and audiences. Children practice various conventions of standard English.

Benchmark Vocabulary

Name ______________________________

DIRECTIONS Write sentences using the words below.

politics popular

Write in Response to Reading

DIRECTIONS Which do you think is the best way to tell about a person's life—an informational text, a story, or a poem? Why? Use details from the texts to support your answer.

Children demonstrate contextual understanding of Benchmark Vocabulary. Children read text closely and use text evidence in their written answers.

Name ______________________________

DIRECTIONS Using text evidence from *Theodore Roosevelt: The Adventurous President,* "Lincoln," and *Marching with Aunt Susan*, follow the directions below.

1. Write several sentences about how Abraham Lincoln, Susan B. Anthony, and Theodore Roosevelt are alike.

2. Select two of the historical figures above and write several sentences about how they are different.

Children analyze and respond to literary and informational text.

Writing

Name ______________________

DIRECTIONS Use the Internet to finish researching the person you chose in Lesson 11. Return to the texts *Theodore Roosevelt: The Adventurous President* and *Marching with Aunt Susan* for examples of good writing. Then, on a separate sheet of paper, write a one or two paragraph first draft about the person you chose. Use facts and details from your research to support your answer.

Conventions

Expand Sentences with Adverbs Rewrite the sentences on the lines below, adding adverbs.

1. Her tooth fell out.

____

2. The birds were singing this morning.

____

3. My teacher led us through the Teddy Roosevelt exhibit.

____

Children write routinely for a range of tasks, purposes, and audiences. Children practice various conventions of standard English.

Name ________________________

Benchmark Vocabulary

DIRECTIONS Write sentences using the words below.

unusual honor

Write in Response to Reading

DIRECTIONS Think about the three texts you have read about important people in American history. Which of these texts had the strongest purpose? Why do you think so? Use evidence from the text to support your opinion.

Children demonstrate contextual understanding of Benchmark Vocabulary. Children read text closely and use text evidence in their written answers.

Name ______________________________

A Few Good Words

It takes many skills to be President of the United States. It is hard work. It has few rewards and can take a little luck, too.

The third President of the United States was Thomas Jefferson. He once said, "I'm a great believer in luck." Abraham Lincoln explained that, "Luck is when preparation meets opportunity." Our fortieth President was Ronald Reagan. He said, "There is no limit to what a man can do if he doesn't mind who gets the credit."

These three Presidents were all different kinds of leaders. They had talents that were special.

Thomas Jefferson had many skills and helped found our country. He was born in 1743 in Virginia. He was an architect, musician, and scientist. He wrote the Declaration of Independence. This paper helped the United States become its own country.

Abraham Lincoln was born in a log cabin in Kentucky in 1809. He later moved to Illinois. He taught himself how to read and study law. As President, he helped free African Americans from slavery.

Before Ronald Reagan became President he was an actor. He was born in Illinois in 1911. He became governor of California. As President he helped make peace with other countries.

Children read text closely to determine what the text says.

Name ______________________

Look for Clues

Underline details in the text that you could use in a biography about one of these men.

Look for Clues: Extend Your Ideas

Choose one of the men in the text. Using clues from the text, write a sentence about the kind of man you think he was.

Ask Questions

Write one question you still have about each president.

Make Your Case

Compare and contrast two presidents. Tell at least one way they were alike and different.

ALIKE: ______________________

DIFFERENT: ______________________

Children read text closely to determine what the text says.

Writing

Name ______________________________

DIRECTIONS Revise and edit your research paper. As you rewrite, look to expand your sentences using descriptive words. Make sure you have included facts and details from your research. Remember that each paragraph should have a topic sentence, supporting details, and a concluding sentence.

Conventions

Expand Sentences with Adjectives and Adverbs Write your own sentences that use adjectives and adverbs.

1. ______________________________

2. ______________________________

Children write routinely for a range of tasks, purposes, and audiences. Children practice various conventions of standard English.

Name ______________________

Long *e* Spelled *e, ee, ea, y*

Pick a word from the box to match each clue. Write the word on the line.
Underline the letters of the word that make the long *e* sound.

beak	bake	sheep	ship
kitty	be	bee	

1. a cat

2. a bird's bill

3. wooly animals

4. a buzzing bug

Read the story. **Underline** words with long *e* spelled *e, ee, ea, y.*

Dad took Bree and me to the beach. We rode in the jeep along the seashore. We parked in the lot and went to the sand. We could feel the heat of the sand on our feet. There was a lot of seaweed on the sand. At the snack bar, I got bean and cheese wraps for Bree and me. I got an iced tea for Dad. He wanted to read his book. Bree wanted to feed her beans to the seagulls. She dropped one on the sand, and a seagull snatched it in his beak. The seagulls were glad we came. So were we.

Children apply grade-level phonics and word analysis skills.

Name ______________________

DIRECTIONS Write sentences using the words below.

community inventor creative

Write in Response to Reading

DIRECTIONS Reread p. 4 of *Change Makers*. What is the main topic of this page? Use details from the text to support your answer.

Children demonstrate contextual understanding of Benchmark Vocabulary. Children read text closely and use text evidence in their written answers.

Name ______________________

Writing

DIRECTIONS Write a paragraph that clearly states and describes the main topic of *Change Makers*. Be sure to include an explanation of how the main topic relates to the title of the unit. Use details from the text to support your answer.

Conventions

Prepositions Circle the preposition in each sentence. Then write your own sentence that uses a preposition.

1. The class took a trip to the zoo.
2. My dad found his lost socks under the bed.
3. ______________________

Children write routinely for a range of tasks, purposes, and audiences. Children practice various conventions of standard English.

Name ______________________

Benchmark Vocabulary

DIRECTIONS Write sentences using the words below.

destroyed harming products

Write in Response to Reading

DIRECTIONS Reread pp. 14–16 of *Change Makers.* What problem did Madison and Rhiannon discover? What did they do about it? Use details from the text to support your answer.

Children demonstrate contextual understanding of Benchmark Vocabulary. Children read text closely and use text evidence in their written answers.

Name ____________________

DIRECTIONS Using evidence from the text, answer the following questions about pp. 12–17 of *Change Makers.*

1. Reread pp. 14–16. What is the connection between Madison and Rhiannon's e-mail campaign and orangutans?

2. Reread p. 17. Why does the author ask if you have products in your home that contain palm oil?

3. Reread p. 9 and p. 15. Do you think there is a connection between the events on these pages? Explain your answer using details from the text.

Children analyze and respond to literary and informational text.

Name ______________________

Writing

DIRECTIONS Write a paragraph that summarizes why Madison and Rhiannon wanted to make a change and what change they made. Identify the text features that helped you write your paragraph. Use examples from the text to support your answer.

Conventions

Using Prepositions Circle the prepositional phrase in the sentence below. Then write your own sentences using prepositional phrases.

1. Our favorite activity is to walk fast in the park.

2. ______________________

3. ______________________

Children write routinely for a range of tasks, purposes, and audiences. Children practice various conventions of standard English.

Name ______________________________

Benchmark Vocabulary

DIRECTIONS Write sentences using the words below.

homeless donated disaster

Write in Response to Reading

DIRECTIONS Reread pp. 22–23 of *Change Makers*. Choose one photo. What part of the text does it help you understand? Use details from the text and photos to support your answer.

Children demonstrate contextual understanding of Benchmark Vocabulary. Children read text closely and use text evidence in their written answers.

Name ______________________________

DIRECTIONS Choose two illustrations in *Change Makers* and write the page number for each one. Then write several sentences that tell how the illustrations help you understand the text, the people, and the setting.

Page ________ : ______________________________

Page ________ : ______________________________

Children analyze and respond to literary and informational text.

Name ______________________

Writing

DIRECTIONS Reread the "Backpacks for Kids" section on p. 20 of *Change Makers.* Draw an illustration that shows Zach giving a backpack to a child. Then write a caption for your illustration.

Conventions

Using Conjunctions Write two of your own sentences that use conjunctions.

1.

2.

Children write routinely for a range of tasks, purposes, and audiences. Children practice various conventions of standard English.

Benchmark Vocabulary

Name ______________________________

DIRECTIONS Write sentences using the words below.

healthy harvest projects

Write in Response to Reading

DIRECTIONS Reread pp. 26–27 of *Change Makers.* What is community action? How do you know? Use examples from the text to support your answer.

Children demonstrate contextual understanding of Benchmark Vocabulary. Children read text closely and use text evidence in their written answers.

Name ______________________

Language Analysis

DIRECTIONS Revisit pp. 24–27 of *Change Makers.* Select a few pages and tell about how these pages help you understand the author's purpose. Use evidence from the text to support your ideas.

Children analyze and respond to literary and informational text.

Name ____________________

Writing

DIRECTIONS Revise the paragraph you wrote in Lesson 2. Be sure to use conjunctions and prepositional phrases correctly. Revisit the text to help you.

Conventions

Using Conjunctions Write sentences to link the subjects below using the conjunctions *and, but,* and *or.*

1. The teacher, his students.

2. sandwich, apple

3. change, country

Children write routinely for a range of tasks, purposes, and audiences. Children practice various conventions of standard English.

Name ______________________________

Benchmark Vocabulary

DIRECTIONS Write sentences using the words below.

champions links

Write in Response to Reading

DIRECTIONS Reread pp. 30–31 of *Change Makers.* How can someone turn an idea into action? Use details from the text to support your answer.

Children demonstrate contextual understanding of Benchmark Vocabulary. Children read text closely and use text evidence in their written answers.

Name ______________________________

DIRECTIONS Using evidence from the text, answer the following questions about pp. 24–31 of *Change Makers.*

1. Revisit pp. 24–25. What reasons does the author provide to support the idea that adults need kids to take action?

2. Reread pp. 28–29. What reasons does the author provide to support the idea that it's important to get involved?

3. Reread pp. 30–31. Which step do you think is most important? Why?

Children analyze and respond to literary and informational text.

Name ____________________

Writing

DIRECTIONS Write a paragraph that summarizes the way young people in *Change Makers* found ways to help their communities. You may use one of the topic sentences suggested in class, but you should include your own concluding sentence.

Conventions

Use Conjunctions Use each pair of verbs in a sentence. Link the verbs using the conjunction *and*.

1. shouted, cheered

2. twirl, leap

Children write routinely for a range of tasks, purposes, and audiences. Children practice various conventions of standard English.

Name ______________________

Long *o* Spelled *o, oa,* and *ow*

cobra boat bow

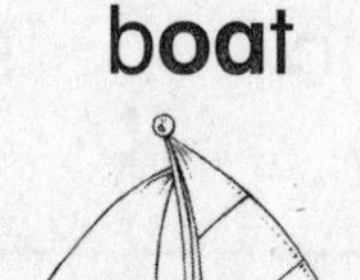

Circle the word in each row with the long *o* sound.
Write the word on the line.

1.	toad	top	two	______
2.	bog	book	bowl	______
3.	took	toss	toast	______
4.	out	over	one	______
5.	most	moss	mop	______
6.	spoon	show	shoe	______
7.	hot	hold	hook	______
8.	play	pot	photo	______
9.	veto	vet	vane	______
10.	good	got	grow	______

Children apply grade-level phonics and word analysis skills.

Name ______________________

Benchmark Vocabulary

DIRECTIONS Write sentences using the words below.

electronic solve

Write in Response to Reading

DIRECTIONS Revisit *Change Makers.* How do the illustrations help you identify the main topic? Use examples from the text to support your answer.

Children demonstrate contextual understanding of Benchmark Vocabulary. Children read text closely and use text evidence in their written answers.

Writing

Name ____________________

DIRECTIONS Choose a teacher, principal, or parent that you would like to interview and plan questions to ask them. Write down three questions that you would ask, but answer them as if you are the person being interviewed. Then write a paragraph, using your answers, that informs people about how that person helps the community.

Conventions

Use Conjunctions Combine the phrases below with the conjunction *and* to make a complete sentence.

1. school was out for the summer

   we made plans to go to the beach

Children write routinely for a range of tasks, purposes, and audiences. Children practice various conventions of standard English.

Name ______________________________

Benchmark Vocabulary

DIRECTIONS Write sentences using the words below.

heap rubble

Write in Response to Reading

DIRECTIONS Reread pp. 137–142 of *City Green.* Why do you think Old Man Hammer is as cranky as he is? Use details from the text to support your answer.

Children demonstrate contextual understanding of Benchmark Vocabulary. Children read text closely and use text evidence in their written answers.

Name ______________________________

DIRECTIONS Using text evidence, answer the following questions about the beginning, middle, and end of *City Green.*

1. List three of your favorite events in chronological order.

2. Reread the last paragraph on p. 148. Why does Marcy's mama tell her that she's making something happen? Use examples from the text to support your answer.

3. Reread p. 162. How has Old Man Hammer changed? Use examples from the text to support your answer.

Children analyze and respond to literary and informational text.

Name ______________________

Writing

DIRECTIONS Think about how the new garden improved Marcy's neighborhood. Then write a paragraph that tells how people in your community might respond to having a neighborhood garden or park. Be sure to include details about how the people in your neighborhood would respond to the garden or park.

Conventions

Adjectives Circle the adjectives in the sentences below.

1. The muddy lot was soon changed into a beautiful garden.
2. When Old Man Hammer sees his little garden, his sour grapes turn sweet.

Children write routinely for a range of tasks, purposes, and audiences. Children practice various conventions of standard English.

Name ______________________________

DIRECTIONS Write sentences using the words below.

packets scoop

DIRECTIONS Reread pp. 140–141 of *City Green*. What does Old Man Hammer see that makes him sad? Use evidence from the text to support your answer.

Children demonstrate contextual understanding of Benchmark Vocabulary. Children read text closely and use text evidence in their written answers.

Name ________________________________

Josh Gibson, Home Run King

Josh Gibson's first love was baseball. In his spare time, Gibson could be found improving his skills and showing off his talent. One night in 1930, Gibson went to watch his hometown team, the Homestead Grays, play against the Kansas City Monarchs. That night changed everything.

The Grays' catcher was injured. The team's owner remembered seeing eighteen-year-old Gibson play ball. He invited the young athlete to play that night. The owner was so impressed that he asked Gibson to join the team. Gibson played professional baseball for the rest of his life.

Josh Gibson was a great player. He hit hundreds of home runs. Gibson led the Negro National League in home runs for ten years. He could hit a baseball harder and farther than almost any other player in the history of the game. He was a skilled catcher too. He earned a place in the Baseball Hall of Fame. But Josh Gibson didn't play in the Major Leagues. The Major Leagues were closed to African American players at the time. Three months after Gibson's death in 1947, Jackie Robinson became the first African American to play in the Major Leagues. He carried on Gibson's tradition of baseball excellence.

Children read text closely to determine what the text says.

Name ______________________________

Look for Clues

Underline details in the text that prove that baseball was important to Josh Gibson.

Look for Clues: Extend Your Ideas

Write a clue that tells why Gibson probably would have wanted to play in the Major Leagues.

____

Ask Questions

Write a question about baseball.

____

Make Your Case

Circle the four facts that you feel were the most important.

Make Your Case: Extend Your Ideas

Write a note to a friend that tells about an important fact you learned.

____

Children read text closely to determine what the text says.

Name ______________________

Writing

DIRECTIONS Write a letter to your city or town and tell them about an idea to improve the community. Use specific details to describe your improvement. Include a diagram or illustration to help your reader understand the plan.

Conventions

Formal and Informal Language Use formal or informal language to answer the questions below.

1. Write the start of a letter to a teacher.

2. Write the start of an e-mail to a friend.

Children write routinely for a range of tasks, purposes, and audiences. Children practice various conventions of standard English.

Benchmark Vocabulary

Name ______________________

DIRECTIONS Write a sentence using the word below.

petition

Write in Response to Reading

DIRECTIONS Reread pp. 144–145. Why does Old Man Hammer refuse to sign the petition? Use details from the text to support your answer.

Children demonstrate contextual understanding of Benchmark Vocabulary. Children read text closely and use text evidence in their written answers.

Name ____________________

DIRECTIONS Look at your Venn Diagram. Think about how Marcy and Old Man Hammer compare to each other as characters. Then write a paragraph that compares and contrasts the two characters' points of view. Remember to include information from your Venn Diagram. Use details from the text to support your answer.

Children analyze and respond to literary and informational text.

Name ______________________________

DIRECTIONS Imagine that you are a visitor to Marcy's neighborhood. Write a paragraph that explains how Marcy's garden changed the neighborhood and why it is important to the community. Use examples from the text to support your answer.

Conventions

Formal and Informal Language Circle the sentence that is written using informal language. Then write why it is informal on the line below.

How are you today, madam?

Yo, how's it goin', dude?

Children write routinely for a range of tasks, purposes, and audiences. Children practice various conventions of standard English.

Name ______________________

Benchmark Vocabulary

DIRECTIONS Write sentences using the words below.

sprinkling patch

Write in Response to Reading

DIRECTIONS Reread pp. 162–163 of *City Green.* What does the illustration tell you about Old Man Hammer's character? Use details from the text to support your answer.

Children demonstrate contextual understanding of Benchmark Vocabulary. Children read text closely and use text evidence in their written answers.

Name ________________________________

DIRECTIONS Using text evidence, answer the following questions about pp. 156–165 of *City Green.*

1. Reread pp. 156–157. How do the illustrations help you understand what is happening?

2. Reread pp. 160–161. How do the illustrations help you visualize the story?

3. Look through pp. 156–165. Write several sentences about an illustration that you would like to add to the story, or about an existing one that you would like to change. Use examples from the text to support your answer.

Children analyze and respond to literary and informational text.

Name ______________________

Writing

DIRECTIONS Design a small garden or park for your neighborhood. Think about the garden in *City Green* for ideas. Write the qualities and characteristics that your garden or park will have. Then tell how it will benefit your neighborhood and community. Remember to include two rules that all visitors must follow.

Conventions

Adjectives Write two sentences that describe you. Circle the adjectives that you use.

Children write routinely for a range of tasks, purposes, and audiences. Children practice various conventions of standard English.

Name ______________________________

Compound Words

Say the word for each picture.
Use two words to make a compound word that names the picture.
Write the compound word on the line.

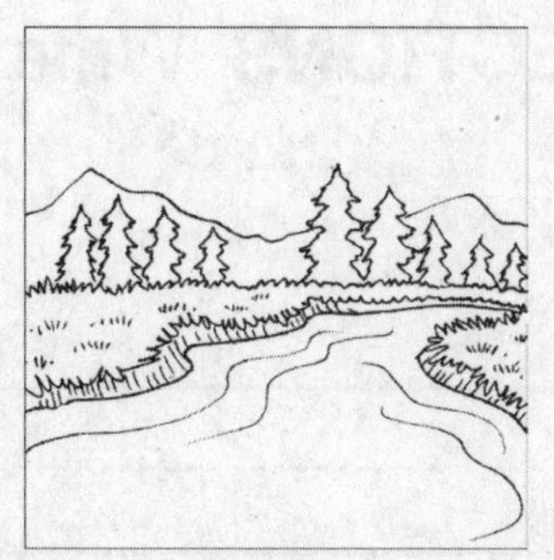

river + bank = riverbank

1. 

spoon pot table tea

____

2. 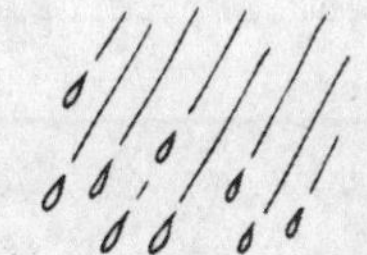

coats drops rain shoes

____

3. 

air box mail plane

____

4. 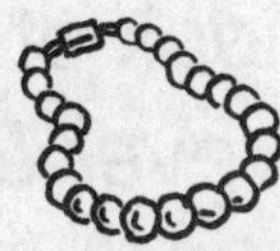

shoe tie lace neck

____

Find the word that you can put together with *meal* to make a compound word.
Mark the space to show your answer.

5. ________ meal

- ○ dinner
- ○ oat
- ○ book

6. meal ________

- ○ time
- ○ spoon
- ○ napkin

Children apply grade-level phonics and word analysis skills.

Name ______________________________

Benchmark Vocabulary

DIRECTIONS Write a sentence using the word below.

undoubtedly

Write in Response to Reading

DIRECTIONS Look at the structure of the poem "City Trees." Then look at the structure of the haikus in *Poems from Cricket Never Does.* Which kind of poem structure do you like better? Why?

Children demonstrate contextual understanding of Benchmark Vocabulary. Children read text closely and use text evidence in their written answers.

Name ____________________

DIRECTIONS Revise your explanation from the previous lesson. Reread your writing, make notes about places you can revise, and then revise your explanation. Then write 1–2 sentences below that summarize how you made your writing stronger.

Formal and Informal Language Circle the formal English examples. Cross out the informal English examples.

Hello!	I'm gonna go to the store.
Yo!	I am going to the store.
She ain't very happy.	She is not very happy.

Children write routinely for a range of tasks, purposes, and audiences. Children practice various conventions of standard English.

Name ______________________________

Benchmark Vocabulary

DIRECTIONS Write sentences using the words below.

healthy harvest petition

Write in Response to Reading

DIRECTIONS Think back over *Change Makers* and *City Green.* Do you think the people discussed in *Change Makers* worked as hard as the characters in *City Green*? Use text evidence to support your answer.

Children demonstrate contextual understanding of Benchmark Vocabulary. Children read text closely and use text evidence in their written answers.

Name ______________________________

DIRECTIONS Reread pp. 24–27 of *Change Makers* and pp. 151–155 of *City Green.* Then write a paragraph that compares the language used in both texts. How is the language similar? How is it different? Use specific details from both texts to support your answer.

Children analyze and respond to literary and informational text.

Name ______________________________

Writing

DIRECTIONS Reread pp. 24–27 of *Change Makers* and pp. 151–155 of *City Green.* Look at the illustrations and note the hard work that people are doing. Write a paragraph that compares how each selection describes hard work. What descriptive words and phrases do the authors use? Use details from both texts to support your answer.

Conventions

Formal and Informal Language Rewrite the sentences below, changing the informal English to formal English.

I can't wait to go on our trip. We're gonna go hiking, dude! The mountain peak is like way up there. Wanna come with?

Children write routinely for a range of tasks, purposes, and audiences. Children practice various conventions of standard English.

Name ______________________

Compound Words

Say the word for each picture.
Use two words to make a compound word.
Write the compound word on the line.

1.

bow coat rain storm

____

2.

bath bird dog house

____

3.

brush hair pick tooth

____

4.

ball base foot print

____

Read the story. **Circle** the compound words.

Reiko was doing her homework by the fireplace. Her eyesight was bad, so she had her eyeglasses on. She heard a footstep outside the window. She picked up her flashlight and went outside to look. Someone had left footprints in the backyard. Reiko went inside. She would have been able to see the footprints better in daylight. Then she saw a man in the moonlight. It was her dad. He had made the footprints. Everything was okay.

Children apply grade-level phonics and word analysis skills.

Name ______________________________

Benchmark Vocabulary

DIRECTIONS Write a sentence using the word below.

dialect

Write in Response to Reading

DIRECTIONS Reread pp. 1–16 of *The Earth Dragon Awakes.* What points of view do the boys have about their fathers? Use examples from the text to support your answer.

Children demonstrate contextual understanding of Benchmark Vocabulary. Children read text closely and use text evidence in their written answers.

Writing

Name ______________________

DIRECTIONS Flag details that reveal Henry's and Chin's points of view about their parents. Then write a scene between Henry and Chin that reveals their points of view. Use thoughts, feelings, and actions to show the point of view of each character.

Conventions

Common and Proper Nouns Circle the common nouns. Cross out the proper nouns. Then write two of your own sentences using common and proper nouns.

1. earthquake San Francisco fire
   umbrella Henry Chin

2. ______________________

3. ______________________

Children write routinely for a range of tasks, purposes, and audiences. Children practice various conventions of standard English.

Name ____________________

Benchmark Vocabulary

DIRECTIONS Write sentences using the words below.

twitches plunges dazed

Write in Response to Reading

DIRECTIONS Reread pp. 17–39 of *The Earth Dragon Awakes.* How does Chin feel when he's buried in the rubble? Use evidence from the text to support your answer.

Children demonstrate contextual understanding of Benchmark Vocabulary. Children read text closely and use text evidence in their written answers.

Name ______________________________

DIRECTIONS Using evidence from the text, answer the following question about pp. 36–39 of *The Earth Dragon Awakes.* Write a few sentences about how the characters in this section respond to the earthquake. What words does the author use to show you how the characters feel?

Children analyze and respond to literary and informational text.

Name ______________________________

Writing

DIRECTIONS Choose a character in the lesson to write about. Then write a paragraph that describes how that character faced the challenges he or she was confronted with during the earthquake.

Conventions

Capitalize Proper Nouns Capitalize the proper nouns in the sentences below. Then write the corrected sentences on the lines.

1. The cable car arrives, and henry climbs on.

2. But fear twists inside chin like a snake.

Children write routinely for a range of tasks, purposes, and audiences. Children practice various conventions of standard English.

Benchmark Vocabulary

Name ______________________________

DIRECTIONS Write sentences using the words below.

scatters missiles

Write in Response to Reading

DIRECTIONS Reread pp. 44–46 of *The Earth Dragon Awakes.* What does Ah Sing do that changes his son's mind about him? Use examples from the text to support your answer.

Children demonstrate contextual understanding of Benchmark Vocabulary. Children read text closely and use text evidence in their written answers.

Name ______________________________

A Real-Life Action Hero

Eric listened closely to the first-aid lesson at his Cub Scout meeting. The guest speaker was talking about the Heimlich maneuver. This action can help someone who is choking. It causes whatever is caught in the choking person's throat to come out. Later Eric saw a television program that taught him more about it. He practiced with his mother. He followed the Cub Scout motto "Be prepared." He had no idea how important that lesson would be.

One day Eric's little sister Jessie was having a snack. Their mother heard Jessie choking. Jessie could not breathe. Nothing their mother did helped.

She called for Eric's help. Then she rushed to call 9-1-1. But Eric was ready. Before his mother could tell the 9-1-1 operator what was happening, Eric sprang into action.

He wrapped his arms around Jessie from behind. He did exactly what he had practiced with his mother. The egg Jessie had been eating popped right out! Jessie was safely breathing again. Ten-year-old Eric was a hero.

Children read text closely to determine what the text says.

Name ______________________________

Look for Clues

Tell why the order of events is important in this story.

____

____

Look for Clues: Extend Your Ideas

Circle words or phrases in the story that help you to follow the order of events.

Ask Questions

Write a question that you have about a home emergency.

____

____

Ask Questions: Extend Your Ideas

Write a question that you would ask Eric about learning such an important safety skill.

____

____

Make Your Case

Tell a friend whether you think the fictional characters make this story more interesting.

____

____

Make Your Case: Extend Your Ideas

Underline a sentence that you found to be most interesting.

Children read text closely to determine what the text says.

Name ______________________

Writing

DIRECTIONS Choose a scene from *The Earth Dragon Awakes.* Then rewrite the scene from Henry's or Chin's point of view. Remember to include dialogue to show their thoughts, feelings, and actions.

Conventions

Identify Singular and Plural Nouns Circle the singular nouns. Cross out the plural nouns. Then write your own sentence that uses a singular or plural noun.

1. books ladder wagon bricks pails houses

2. carts door horses rivers nails rock

3.

Children write routinely for a range of tasks, purposes, and audiences. Children practice various conventions of standard English.

Benchmark Vocabulary

Name ______________________________

DIRECTIONS Write sentences using the words below.

surges trample

Write in Response to Reading

DIRECTIONS Revisit pp. 62–81 of *The Earth Dragon Awakes.* Choose a character from this section whom you think is a hero. What is it about that character's response to events that makes him or her a hero? Use evidence from the text to support your answer.

Children demonstrate contextual understanding of Benchmark Vocabulary. Children read text closely and use text evidence in their written answers.

Name ______________________

DIRECTIONS Revisit pp. 62–81 of *The Earth Dragon Awakes.* Choose two characters from this section and write a paragraph that compares and contrasts each character's response to the earthquake. Use evidence from the text to support your answer.

Children analyze and respond to literary and informational text.

Writing

Name ______________________________

DIRECTIONS Choose one character and one event from pp. 62–81 of *The Earth Dragon Awakes.* Then write a narrative paragraph about the actions that character took in response to the event. Use evidence from the text to support your answer.

Conventions

Identify Irregular Plural Nouns Write two of your own sentences that use irregular plural nouns.

1. ______________________________

2. ______________________________

Children write routinely for a range of tasks, purposes, and audiences.
Children practice various conventions of standard English.

Name ______________________________

Benchmark Vocabulary

DIRECTIONS Write sentences using the words below.

revenge parched

Write in Response to Reading

DIRECTIONS Reread pp. 102–105 of *The Earth Dragon Awakes.* What happens at the end of the story? Use key details from the text to support your answer.

Children demonstrate contextual understanding of Benchmark Vocabulary. Children read text closely and use text evidence in their written answers.

Name ______________________

DIRECTIONS Using evidence from the text, answer the following questions about pp. 82–105 of *The Earth Dragon Awakes.*

1. Reread pp. 89–92. Write several sentences about the Great Fire. What events happened that made this fire so large and terrible? Use evidence from the text to support your answer.

2. Reread pp. 96–99. Summarize the events that take place in this section. What do the people of San Francisco do to control the fire? Use specific details from the text to support your answer.

Children analyze and respond to literary and informational text.

Name ______________________________

Writing

DIRECTIONS Choose a scene from *The Earth Dragon Awakes* to expand upon. Use temporal words to tell the sequence of the events. Remember to wrap up your scene with a conclusion.

Conventions

Identify Collective Nouns Circle the collective nouns. Then write your own sentence about *The Earth Dragon Awakes* that uses a collective noun.

1. person family team student crew

2.

Children write routinely for a range of tasks, purposes, and audiences. Children practice various conventions of standard English.

Name ______________________________

Long *i* Spelled *i, ie, igh, y*

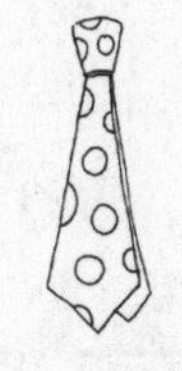

child night cry tie

Circle a word to finish each sentence.

1. Things seem darker after you look at something ______________.

   bite bring bright

2. You can ______________ out for yourself.

   fin find fight

3. Put some gray paper ______________ some black paper.

   bit by bite

4. Put it ______________ next to white paper.

   rid right rye

Read the first word. **Circle** the word in each row with the same vowel sound as the first word.

5. spider: tiger trigger ticket
6. pie: undo unlock untie
7. light: finger finish fright
8. fly: shy ship shin

Children apply grade-level phonics and word analysis skills.

Name ______________________________

Benchmark Vocabulary

DIRECTIONS Write sentences using the words below.

insurance ruins

Write in Response to Reading

DIRECTIONS Reread pp. 107–117 of *The Earth Dragon Awakes.* Write several sentences about two connections that you made between the story and the facts in the Afterword. Use evidence from the text to explain the connections.

Children demonstrate contextual understanding of Benchmark Vocabulary. Children read text closely and use text evidence in their written answers.

Writing

Name ______________________

DIRECTIONS Write a sequence of events from Henry's or Chin's life that is connected to a historical or scientific event. Use temporal words to signal the order of events. Remember to revisit the Afterword to find historical and scientific facts about the earthquake.

Conventions

Past and Present Verb Tense Change each present tense verb to past tense. Then write your own present and past tense verbs.

1. skates ____________

2. bakes ____________

3. ____________

4. ____________

Children write routinely for a range of tasks, purposes, and audiences. Children practice various conventions of standard English.

Name ______________________

Benchmark Vocabulary

DIRECTIONS Write sentences using the words below.

confidence courage

Write in Response to Reading

DIRECTIONS Reread pp. 102–105 of *The Earth Dragon Awakes.* How does the ending of the book relate to the author's central message? Use evidence from the text to support your answer.

Children demonstrate contextual understanding of Benchmark Vocabulary. Children read text closely and use text evidence in their written answers.

Name ______________________________

DIRECTIONS Using evidence from the text, answer the following questions about *The Earth Dragon Awakes.*

1. What is a central message?

2. Think back to the events of *The Earth Dragon Awakes.* Choose three events from the text and explain how they contribute to the central message. Use specific details and evidence to support your answer.

Children analyze and respond to literary and informational text.

Name ____________________

Writing

DIRECTIONS On a separate sheet of paper, write a scene from either Henry's or Chin's point of view that tells the central message of the story. Include details about how the character feels and what he is thinking. Describe the character's actions. Revisit *The Earth Dragon Awakes* to look for examples of how the author shows what a character is feeling and thinking.

Conventions

Nouns and Verbs Underline the nouns. Circle the verbs. Then write your own sentence. Remember to underline the noun and circle the verb.

1. The fire spread quickly.
2. The dog howled loudly.
3. The Great Earthquake and Fire destroyed more than 28,000 houses, stores, and other buildings.

____

4. ____________________

____

Children write routinely for a range of tasks, purposes, and audiences. Children practice various conventions of standard English.

Benchmark Vocabulary

Name ______________________________

DIRECTIONS Write sentences using the words below.

fortune advised

Write in Response to Reading

DIRECTIONS Reread pp. 5–11 of *Seek the Sun.* Whose point of view do you most agree with—the sandalmaker or the builder? Use evidence from the text to support your answer.

Children demonstrate contextual understanding of Benchmark Vocabulary. Children read text closely and use text evidence in their written answers.

Name ______________________

Writing

DIRECTIONS Think about the points of view of the builder and the people affected by the building's shadow. On a separate sheet of paper, write a story scene that expresses the builder's or the neighbor's point of view. Revisit pp. 7–8 of *Seek the Sun* to find evidence of thoughts, feelings, and actions that reveal the character's point of view. Then, use this evidence to help reveal the character's point of view in your scene.

Conventions

Irregular Verbs Write the underlined present tense verb as a past tense verb.

1. I eat cereal for breakfast.

____

2. She builds a fence around the building.

____

3. They find a crowd of angry people.

____

Children write routinely for a range of tasks, purposes, and audiences. Children practice various conventions of standard English.

Name ______________________________

Benchmark Vocabulary

DIRECTIONS Write sentences using the words below.

tended lovingly precious

Write in Response to Reading

DIRECTIONS Reread pp. 5–8 of *Seek the Sun*. Do you think it would have been understandable if the sandalmaker's wife had gotten just as upset as her husband? Use evidence from the text to support your answer.

Children demonstrate contextual understanding of Benchmark Vocabulary. Children read text closely and use text evidence in their written answers.

Name ________________________________

DIRECTIONS Reread pp. 7–8 of *Seek the Sun.* Find details in this section that tell how both the sandalmaker **and** his wife responded to the tall building. Then write these details on the lines below.

Children analyze and respond to literary and informational text.

Name ________________________

Writing

DIRECTIONS Consider the responses of the sandalmaker and his wife in the story. Flag text evidence that reveals how each character responded to a challenge. On a separate sheet of paper, describe how each character responded to the challenge they faced. Use thoughts, feelings, and actions to reveal and describe how they responded.

Conventions

Irregular Verbs Read the present tense verbs. Cross out the incorrect past tense verbs. Then write two of your own sentences using irregular past tense verbs.

1.

Present Tense	Past Tense	Past Tense
swim keep	swam keeped	swimmed kept

2. ________________________

3. ________________________

Children write routinely for a range of tasks, purposes, and audiences. Children practice various conventions of standard English.

Name ________________________________

Benchmark Vocabulary

DIRECTIONS Write sentences using the words below.

essential protected

Write in Response to Reading

DIRECTIONS Reread pp. 8–11 of *Seek the Sun*. Do you think knowing that the story is based on a real court case makes it better? Explain why or why not.

Children demonstrate contextual understanding of Benchmark Vocabulary. Children read text closely and use text evidence in their written answers.

Name ______________________________

DIRECTIONS Write a description of the park at the end of *Seek the Sun*. Tell how the author's description of the park helps to provide closure for the reader. Use evidence from the text to support your answer.

Children analyze and respond to literary and informational text.

Name ______________________

Writing

DIRECTIONS Choose six events from the story and flag text evidence that describes each event. On a separate sheet of paper, write a sentence that describes each event. Remember that your description of each event must include evidence from the text. Then, use these descriptions to create a storyboard. Make your pictures as detailed as possible to support your sentences.

Conventions

Irregular Verbs Write the past tense verb for each present tense verb.

1. see ______________

2. come ______________

3. sing ______________

4. catch ______________

Children write routinely for a range of tasks, purposes, and audiences. Children practice various conventions of standard English.

Name ______________________________

Comparative Endings *-er, -est*

Circle a word to finish each sentence.
Write the word on the line.

Spot is **big.**
Rover is **bigger.**
Spike is **biggest.**

smaller smallest

1. The spotted one is the __________________.

taller tallest

2. Nate is __________________ than Jack.

happier happiest

3. Ben is __________________ than Josh.

wetter wettest

4. Jill is the __________________ of all.

fatter fattest

5. This clown is __________________ than that one.

Children apply grade-level phonics and word analysis skills.

Name ________________________________

Benchmark Vocabulary

DIRECTIONS Write sentences using the words below.

shiver vanish tremble faint

Write in Response to Reading

DIRECTIONS Reread "The Fool on the Hill" and "Mother of the Mountains." Why do you think cultures told myths about the same subject, such as thunder? Use evidence from both texts to support your answer.

Children demonstrate contextual understanding of Benchmark Vocabulary. Children read text closely and use text evidence in their written answers.

Writing

Name ______________________

DIRECTIONS Think of another version of a myth about what causes thunder. On a separate sheet of paper, list the ideas, thoughts, feelings, and actions that your characters might engage in. Then write a first draft of your myth.

Conventions

Identify and Use Subject Pronouns Write your own sentences that use subject pronouns.

1. ______________________

2. ______________________

Children write routinely for a range of tasks, purposes, and audiences. Children practice various conventions of standard English.

Name ______________________

Benchmark Vocabulary

DIRECTIONS Write sentences using the words below.

dialect precious

Write in Response to Reading

DIRECTIONS Revisit pp. 12–15 of *The Earth Dragon Awakes* and pp. 5–7 of *Seek the Sun*. What is similar about the dragon imagery in these stories? What is different? Use evidence from both texts to support your answers.

Children demonstrate contextual understanding of Benchmark Vocabulary. Children read text closely and use text evidence in their written answers.

Name ______________________________

DIRECTIONS Think about how people from different cultures may speak different languages and have different customs, habits, foods, and jobs. List ways the characters in *The Earth Dragon Awakes* and *Seek the Sun* are both alike and different. Use evidence from both texts to help you create your lists.

Children analyze and respond to literary and informational text.

Name ______________________

Writing

DIRECTIONS Determine how you want your myth about what causes thunder to end. Craft a conclusion to your myth about what causes thunder. Then revise and edit your conclusion to address only the key details that are significant.

Conventions

Object Pronouns Use an object pronoun to complete the sentences below. Then write your own sentence using an object pronoun.

1. Students went to the library. Their parents went with __________.

2. My brother is making a mess. Mom asked __________ to clean it up.

3. ______________________

Children write routinely for a range of tasks, purposes, and audiences.Children practice various conventions of standard English.

Benchmark Vocabulary

Name ______________________________

DIRECTIONS Write sentences using the words below.

surges essential

Write in Response to Reading

DIRECTIONS Write several sentences about the importance of the author's notes at the end of both *The Earth Dragon Awakes* and *Seek the Sun*. Use evidence from both texts to support your answer.

Children demonstrate contextual understanding of Benchmark Vocabulary. Children read text closely and use text evidence in their written answers.

Name ______________________________

The Blank Book

Elias's dad was in the army. He was leaving home to be stationed in another country. As he said good-bye, Dad gave Elias a book. "I want you to read this when you get home," Dad said.

Elias didn't feel like reading, but he opened the book anyway...and what a surprise! Every page was blank except the first one. There, Dad explained that they would take turns writing in the book, mailing it back and forth while Dad was gone.

Elias began writing immediately, telling his dad how much he missed him, and then he mailed the book. Three weeks later, the book came back. Dad wrote about a market he had visited. He described the sharp, spicy smells and bright, patterned carpets. He described the warm, buttery bread he tried.

Elias and his dad wrote often. Dad described what life was like on the base. Sometimes he invented silly stories or drew neat pictures. Elias wrote about home and school. He drew colorful pictures. They had to get another book before long, and then another!

When Dad came home, he had a new book with him. "I thought we could keep going," Dad said, grinning. Elias nodded. This was definitely a tradition he wanted to keep.

Children read text closely to determine what the text says.

Name ______________________________

Look for Clues

Underline clues that show similarities between what Dad and Elias wrote. Circle clues that show differences between what they wrote.

Look for Clues: Extend Your Ideas

Star the sentence that tells how Elias felt when his dad first gave the book to him.

Ask Questions

Write a question you might ask Dad about where he is living.

____

Ask Questions: Extend Your Ideas

Write a question Dad might ask Elias about school.

____

Make Your Case

On a separate sheet of paper, write two things that could be actual events in the story. Tell why you believe they could be actual events.

Make Your Case: Extend Your Ideas

Highlight descriptive words the author uses to add to the fictional story.

Children read text closely to determine what the text says.

Name ______________________

Writing

DIRECTIONS Reread your revised draft several times. Check the spelling of any words that your partner circled. Then use the editing checklist compiled by your classmates to edit your revised draft.

Conventions

Identify Reflexive Pronouns Use a reflexive pronoun to complete the sentences below. Then write your own sentence that uses a reflexive pronoun.

1. As I prepared for my spelling test, I told ______________________ to remain calm.
2. Because he was early for the movie, he had time to get ______________________ set up with popcorn.
3. ______________________

Children write routinely for a range of tasks, purposes, and audiences. Children practice various conventions of standard English.

Name ______________________________

Final Syllable *-le*

ankle	bubble	bugle	people	table	turtle

Say the word for each picture.
Write the word on the line.
Use the words in the box if you need help.

app<u>le</u>

1. ____________	2. ____________	3. ____________
4. ____________	5 ____________	6. ____________

Circle the word in each sentence that ends with the same sound as *apple*.

7. José took a tumble when he tripped on the branch.

8. I got a new puzzle for my birthday.

9. Can you read the title of this book?

Children apply grade-level phonics and word analysis skills.

Name ______________________________

Benchmark Vocabulary

DIRECTIONS Write sentences using the words below.

rotating violent alerts

Write in Response to Reading

DIRECTIONS Reread the first paragraph on p. 5 of *Disaster Alert!* What is the focus of this paragraph? Use examples from the text to support your answer.

Children demonstrate contextual understanding of Benchmark Vocabulary. Children read text closely and use text evidence in their written answers.

Name ______________________

DIRECTIONS Choose a topic about tornadoes from pp. 4–9 of *Disaster Alert!* Write an informative paragraph that introduces the tornado-related topic and supports it with details. Use examples from the text to support your answer.

Use Adjectives Underline the adjectives in the sentences below.

1. It was a cool, rainy day.
2. The sky was dark.
3. The vegetable was smelly and green.

Children write routinely for a range of tasks, purposes, and audiences. Children practice various conventions of standard English.

Name ______________________________

Benchmark Vocabulary

DIRECTIONS Write sentences using the words below.

absorb electrical

Write in Response to Reading

DIRECTIONS Reread p. 11 of *Disaster Alert!* What happened in Tewkesbury, Gloucestershire, England in 2007? Use examples from the text to support your answer.

Children demonstrate contextual understanding of Benchmark Vocabulary. Children read text closely and use text evidence in their written answers.

Name ______________________________

DIRECTIONS Reread pp. 12–13 of *Disaster Alert!* Write a few sentences that tell about the main topic of this section. Use evidence from the text to help you identify what the main topic is.

Children analyze and respond to literary and informational text.

Name ______________________

Writing

DIRECTIONS Review the paragraph you wrote in Lesson 1. Look for any terms that might require a definition. Use the sources provided to look up any definitions and to search for more details that might add to readers' understanding of your paragraph. Then add this information into your paragraph.

Conventions

Use Adjectives Write two of your own sentences that use adjectives on the lines below.

1. ______________________

2. ______________________

Children write routinely for a range of tasks, purposes, and audiences. Children practice various conventions of standard English.

Benchmark Vocabulary

Name ______________________

DIRECTIONS Write sentences using the words below.

dissolves collapse explore

Write in Response to Reading

DIRECTIONS Reread pp. 18–19 of *Disaster Alert!* What reasons support the author's point that some sinkholes collapse quickly and without warning? Use examples from the text to support your answer.

Children demonstrate contextual understanding of Benchmark Vocabulary. Children read text closely and use text evidence in their written answers.

Name ______________________

Writing

DIRECTIONS Choose a topic from the list of natural disasters provided by your teacher, or from an idea of your own. Research facts and definitions related to your chosen natural disaster. Then write an informative/explanatory paragraph about your topic using facts and definitions from your research.

Conventions

Use Adjectives Circle the adjective. Tell which word the adjective describes.

1. The rocky plates below the ground move slowly.

2. This creates a violent storm called a supercell.

Children write routinely for a range of tasks, purposes, and audiences. Children practice various conventions of standard English.

Benchmark Vocabulary

Name ______________________________

DIRECTIONS Write sentences using the words below.

pressure erupts poisons

Write in Response to Reading

DIRECTIONS Reread p. 27 of *Disaster Alert!* What does the word *dormant* mean? How does knowing the meaning of the word help you learn about volcanoes? Use details from the text to support your answer.

Children demonstrate contextual understanding of Benchmark Vocabulary. Children read text closely and use text evidence in their written answers.

Name ______________________

Language Analysis

DIRECTIONS Using evidence from the text, answer the following questions about pp. 22–27 of *Disaster Alert!*

1. Reread pp. 22–23. What escapes to the Earth's surface when a volcano erupts?

2. Where is the tallest volcano in the solar system located?

3. Reread pp. 24–25. What should you do if a volcano erupts near you?

4. Reread pp. 26–27. What does a volcanologist do?

5. Reread pp. 26–27. What does it mean to say that a volcano is *extinct*?

Children analyze and respond to literary and informational text.

Name ______________________

Writing

DIRECTIONS Write a descriptive paragraph about a change caused by a natural event. Your paragraph should include at least two challenges this change caused for people. Introduce your topic, list at least two challenges, and write a concluding statement. Use descriptive words so your reader will be able to picture the change and the challenges it caused.

Conventions

Adjectives Write two of your own sentences about a natural disaster. Circle the adjectives. Use information from pp. 22–27 of *Disaster Alert!* to help you.

1. ______________________

2. ______________________

Children write routinely for a range of tasks, purposes, and audiences. Children practice various conventions of standard English.

Name ______________________________

Benchmark Vocabulary

DIRECTIONS Write sentences using the words below.

faulty extreme shelters

Write in Response to Reading

DIRECTIONS Reread pp. 28–29 of *Disaster Alert!* What is a bushfire? Use details from the text to support your answer.

Children demonstrate contextual understanding of Benchmark Vocabulary. Children read text closely and use text evidence in their written answers.

Name ______________________________

DIRECTIONS Using evidence from the text, answer the following questions about pp. 28–31 of *Disaster Alert!*

1. Why is it important to describe connections between scientific ideas in a text?

2. Reread pp. 28–30. Write a few sentences about why you think bushfires caused so much destruction in Australia. Use evidence from the text to support your answer.

Children analyze and respond to literary and informational text.

Name ______________________________

Writing

DIRECTIONS Revisit *Disaster Alert!* and collect key details from the text, illustrations, and diagrams. On a separate sheet of paper, organize your main ideas and details by creating a Main Idea and Details chart. Choose a central idea. Add your key ideas and details to your chart. Then write a summary based on the information in your chart.

Conventions

Adjectives Circle the adjectives. Then write your own sentence that includes two different adjectives.

1. The ground shook. I crawled under the wooden table for protection. My sister let out a loud screech. My calming words helped her. Earthquakes are scary!

2. ______________________________

Children write routinely for a range of tasks, purposes, and audiences. Children practice various conventions of standard English.

Name ____________________

Vowel Patterns *oo, u*

 c<u>oo</u>k	 b<u>u</u>ll

full	hood	hook	pull	shook	stood	took	wood

Write three words from the box that rhyme with **good**.

1. ________	2. ________	3. ________

Write three words from the box that rhyme with **look.**

4. ________	5. ________	6. ________

Write a word from the box that is the opposite of each word below.

7. push	8. empty
________	________

Write a word from the box to finish each sentence.

brook	put

9. I ________ a hook on the fishing pole.

10. I pulled a fish from the ________.

Children apply grade-level phonics and word analysis skills.

Name ______________________________

Benchmark Vocabulary

DIRECTIONS Write sentences using the words below.

damage wreck

Write in Response to Reading

DIRECTIONS Revisit pp. 12–43 of *Danger! Earthquakes.* How does the title of the text help you identify the main topic? Use evidence from the text to support your answer.

Children demonstrate contextual understanding of Benchmark Vocabulary. Children read text closely and use text evidence in their written answers.

Name ________________________

DIRECTIONS Choose two earthquakes from *Danger! Earthquakes* to compare. Then write an informative/explanatory paragraph that uses key ideas and details from the text to help you compare them. Introduce your topic and develop your main points using key ideas and facts. Remember to provide a concluding statement.

Adverbs Underline the adverb in the sentence below. Then write your own sentence about earthquakes that uses an adverb.

1. I finished my homework easily.

2. ________________________

Children write routinely for a range of tasks, purposes, and audiences. Children practice various conventions of standard English.

Name ______________________________

Benchmark Vocabulary

DIRECTIONS Write sentences using the words below.

measure   level   recorded

Write in Response to Reading

DIRECTIONS Reread pp. 14–15 of *Danger! Earthquakes.* Do the images on these pages help you understand the text? Use evidence from the text to support your answer.

Children demonstrate contextual understanding of Benchmark Vocabulary. Children read text closely and use text evidence in their written answers.

Name ______________________________

DIRECTIONS Write several sentences that tell how the map on pp. 22–23 helps you to understand the text better.

Children analyze and respond to literary and informational text.

Name ______________________________

Writing

DIRECTIONS Revisit the map on pp. 22–23 of *Danger! Earthquakes.* Write two questions you have that can be answered by the map. Then answer those questions on the lines below using facts and definitions.

Conventions

Adverbs Add an adverb to describe the verb.

1. The earthquake shook San Francisco ____________.

2. Ports were ____________ destroyed by giant waves.

Children write routinely for a range of tasks, purposes, and audiences. Children practice various conventions of standard English.

Name ______________________________

DIRECTIONS Write a sentence using the word below.

grind

DIRECTIONS Revisit pp. 24–33 of *Danger! Earthquakes.* Describe the connection between two scientific ideas from this section. Use evidence from the text to support your answer.

Children demonstrate contextual understanding of Benchmark Vocabulary. Children read text closely and use text evidence in their written answers.

Name ______________________

Curtis the Cowboy Cook

Curtis was bored and unhappy. He thought when he was hired to work on the cattle drive that he'd finally get to be a real cowboy. But the cowboys treated him like a kid. The cook, Dusty, let Curtis help him. But Dusty was so busy he barely had time to talk. Curtis just watched and did chores for the cook all day long.

The chuckwagon always went ahead of the slow-moving cattle. That way, dinner would be ready when the cowboys got to camp each night. Dusty and Curtis started the cooking fire. As they carried water from a creek, Dusty slipped down the bank. He landed hard. Curtis helped Dusty limp painfully to camp. Then Curtis got to work with Dusty directing him.

He cut the salt pork and arranged it in deep pans. He scooped beans into the pans, covered them with water, and set them on the fire to boil. Soon the contents of the pans were bubbling, and the smell filled the camp. As the sun went down, the tired, hungry cowboys arrived. One bite of the hearty pork and beans was enough to convince them that Curtis was born to be a cowboy cook.

Children read text closely to determine what the text says.

Name ____________________

Look for Clues

Underline details that tell how the cowboys first felt about Curtis. Highlight details that tell how the cowboys' feelings changed about Curtis.

Look for Clues: Extend Your Ideas

Circle clues that tell how Curtis feels at the beginning of the story.

Ask Questions

Write a question you have about cowboys.

____

Ask Questions: Extend Your Ideas

Ask a partner a question you might ask the cowboys about their actions towards Curtis.

Make Your Case

On a separate sheet of paper, list activities from the story that real cowboys do. Tell which one you think is most interesting and why.

____

Make Your Case: Extend Your Ideas

On a separate sheet of paper, write an e-mail to a friend about your thoughts about being a cowboy.

Children read text closely to determine what the text says.

Name ______________________________

Writing

DIRECTIONS Decide on a natural disaster that you would like to research. On a separate sheet of paper, take notes that answer the questions *who, what, where, when,* and *why*. Then write an informative/explanatory paragraph on the lines below that explains the answers to these questions.

Conventions

Adverbs Write two of your own sentences that include an adverb. Underline the adverb. Circle the verb it describes.

1. ______________________________

2. ______________________________

Children write routinely for a range of tasks, purposes, and audiences. Children practice various conventions of standard English.

Name ______________________________

Benchmark Vocabulary

DIRECTIONS Write sentences using the words below.

collapse steep loose

Write in Response to Reading

DIRECTIONS Reread p. 31 and pp. 38–39 of *Disaster! Earthquakes*. How do the details on pp. 38–39 support the author's points on p. 31? Explain your answer using evidence from the text.

Children demonstrate contextual understanding of Benchmark Vocabulary. Children read text closely and use text evidence in their written answers.

Name ______________________

DIRECTIONS Using evidence from the text, answer the following questions about pp. 38–39 of *Danger! Earthquakes.*

1. Where do most earthquakes occur?

2. What do the colors on the map mean?

3. What is your favorite feature on the map? Explain why that feature is your favorite.

Children analyze and respond to literary and informational text.

Writing

Name ______________________________

DIRECTIONS Write a conclusion for the natural disaster paragraph you wrote in the previous lesson.

Conventions

Adverbs Write three of your own sentences using adverbs. Use adverbs that you have not used before.

1. ______________________________

2. ______________________________

3. ______________________________

Children write routinely for a range of tasks, purposes, and audiences. Children practice various conventions of standard English.

Name ______________________

Benchmark Vocabulary

DIRECTIONS Write a sentence using the word below.

divide

Write in Response to Reading

DIRECTIONS Reread "Who Could Somersault the San Andreas Fault?" Why do you think the poet took a humorous approach to such a serious topic? Use evidence from the text to support your answer.

Children demonstrate contextual understanding of Benchmark Vocabulary. Children read text closely and use text evidence in their written answers.

Name ______________________

DIRECTIONS Using evidence from the text, answer the following questions about "Who Could Somersault the San Andreas Fault?"

1. Why do you think poets choose to use words that rhyme?

____

____

2. Why do you think the poet says, "I think *I'll* stay in bed and sleep"?

____

____

3. Do you think there are actual road signs that say: "NO JUMPING OVER CALIFORNIA!"

____

____

Children analyze and respond to literary and informational text.

Name ______________________

Writing

DIRECTIONS Write several sentences about a fact you have learned about one kind of natural disaster. Revisit the texts to choose a fact that interests you. Remember to clearly state the fact you are writing about. Use different words than the text uses to describe your ideas.

Conventions

Apostrophes in Contractions Rewrite each word pair as a contraction. Then write your own sentence that uses a contraction.

1. She will ______________ **2.** They are ______________

3. ______________________________

Children write routinely for a range of tasks, purposes, and audiences. Children practice various conventions of standard English.

Name ______________________________

Diphthongs *ou, ow, oi, oy*

house

cow

coin

toy

Read the name of the picture. **Circle** the word that has the same vowel sound as the name of the picture.

1. clown — power, point, pot	**2.** boy — soybean, town, robe
3. boil — owl, oil, allow	**4.** mouse — join, loyal, loud

Pick a word from the box to finish each sentence. **Write** the word on the line.

town
about
join
enjoy

5. We ______________ this game.

6. We are the best team in ______________.

7. You can ______________ us in the game.

8. We play ______________ once a week.

Children apply grade-level phonics and word analysis skills.

Name ______________________

Benchmark Vocabulary

DIRECTIONS Write a sentence using the word below.

grind

Write in Response to Reading

DIRECTIONS Revisit pp. 16–17 of *Disaster Alert!* and pp. 30–31 of *Danger! Earthquakes*. What do the sections of these texts have in common? Use examples from both texts to support your answer.

Children demonstrate contextual understanding of Benchmark Vocabulary. Children read text closely and use text evidence in their written answers.

Name ______________________________

DIRECTIONS Choose an event from *Disaster Alert!* or *Danger! Earthquake.* Research the event to answer the questions *who, what, where, when,* and *why*. Then write your newspaper article on the lines below. Remember to include a headline that clearly states the event you are writing about.

Contractions List five contractions on the lines below.

Children write routinely for a range of tasks, purposes, and audiences. Children practice various conventions of standard English.

Name ______________________________

Benchmark Vocabulary

DIRECTIONS Write sentences using the words below.

collapse damage

Write in Response to Reading

DIRECTIONS Think back to *Disaster Alert!* and *Danger! Earthquakes*. Which informational text is more helpful for finding information? Use evidence from both texts to support your answer.

Children demonstrate contextual understanding of Benchmark Vocabulary. Children read text closely and use text evidence in their written answers.

Name ______________________________

DIRECTIONS Write two comparison statements and two contrast statements about the text structures of *Danger! Earthquakes* and *Disaster Alert!* Revisit both texts to look for details. Use these details to support your answer.

Name ______________________

Writing

DIRECTIONS Revise the newspaper article you wrote in the previous lesson. Look for errors in spelling, punctuation, and capitalization. Think about information that you might like to add.

Conventions

Contractions Write three of your own sentences that use contractions.

1. ______________________

2. ______________________

3. ______________________

Children write routinely for a range of tasks, purposes, and audiences. Children practice various conventions of standard English.

Name ______________________

Syllable Patterns

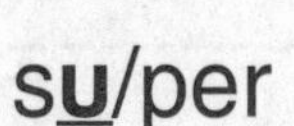

su/per

sup/per

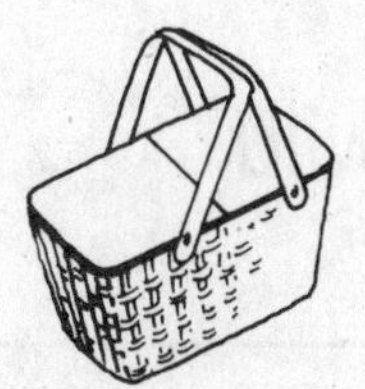

bas/ket

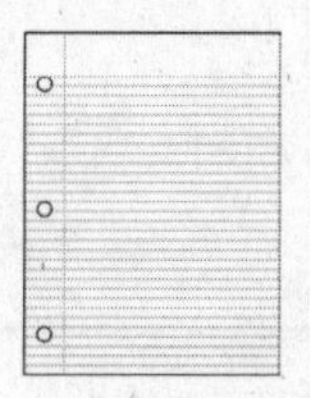

pa/per

Pick a word from the box to match each clue.
Write the word on the line.

cowboy	magnet	picnic	blanket	painting
begin	tiger	oatmeal	boyhood	joyful

1. This is a wild animal. ______________
2. Some people eat this for breakfast. ______________
3. This is the same as happy. ______________
4. A nail sticks to this. ______________
5. This is when you eat outside in the park. ______________
6. He rides a horse and herds cows. ______________
7. This can keep you warm in bed. ______________
8. This word is opposite of **end**. ______________

Children apply grade-level phonics and word analysis skills.

Name ______________________________

Benchmark Vocabulary

DIRECTIONS Write sentences using the words below.

wild tangled

Write in Response to Reading

DIRECTIONS Reread pp. 3–6 of *John Chapman: Planter and Pioneer.* What is the main topic of this biography? Use details from the text to support your answer.

Children demonstrate contextual understanding of Benchmark Vocabulary. Children read text closely and use text evidence in their written answers.

Name ______________________________

Writing

DIRECTIONS Revisit the illustrations on pp. 3–6 of *John Chapman: Planter and Pioneer.* Write a paragraph that explains whether you think there is enough evidence to support the idea that Johnny Appleseed was an important figure. Use reasons and evidence from the text and illustrations to support your answer.

Conventions

Apostrophes in Singular Possessives Complete the sentences below with singular possessive nouns.

1. ______________ dad knew that he loved the outdoors.

2. ______________ favorite thing was the way plants grew so thick and tangled.

Children write routinely for a range of tasks, purposes, and audiences. Children practice various conventions of standard English.

Name ______________________

Benchmark Vocabulary

DIRECTIONS Write sentences using the words below.

amazed visitors

Write in Response to Reading

DIRECTIONS Reread pp. 7–10 of *John Chapman: Planter and Pioneer.* Would you want to live back in the time of Johnny Appleseed? Use evidence from the text to support your answer.

Children demonstrate contextual understanding of Benchmark Vocabulary. Children read text closely and use text evidence in their written answers.

Name ______________________________

DIRECTIONS Using evidence from the text, answer the following questions about pp. 7–10 of *John Chapman: Planter and Pioneer.*

1. Reread p. 7. Where did John sleep at night?

2. Reread pp. 8–10. What did John eat?

3. What amazed visitors about John?

4. Why did John choose to not wear shoes?

Children analyze and respond to literary and informational text.

Name ______________________________

Writing

DIRECTIONS Revisit pp. 7–10 of *John Chapman: Planter and Pioneer.* Write a paragraph that explores the connection between the title of the book and the unit title – Pioneering New Ideas and New Worlds. Use reasons and evidence from the text to support your answer.

Conventions

Apostrophes in Plural Possessives Write two of your own sentences that use plural possessives.

1.

2.

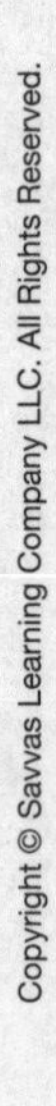

Children write routinely for a range of tasks, purposes, and audiences. Children practice various conventions of standard English.

Name ______________________________

DIRECTIONS Write a sentence using the word below.

beneath

DIRECTIONS Reread the first paragraph on p. 15 of *John Chapman: Planter and Pioneer.* What is the main purpose of this paragraph? What details support the main purpose? Use examples from the text to support your answer.

Children demonstrate contextual understanding of Benchmark Vocabulary. Children read text closely and use text evidence in their written answers.

Name ____________________________

Sleuth Passage

Journey to Freedom

In 1854, William was an African American slave in North Carolina. He longed to be free, but that did not seem possible. Late one night, a friend woke up William. He wanted William to escape with him to Canada.

The thought of freedom made William joyful. But how would he and his friend get to Canada? It was hundreds of miles away. They had very little money or food. They had no maps. Where would they hide along the way? Soldiers and other people were looking everywhere for runaway slaves. The answer to his questions was the Underground Railroad.

The Underground Railroad was not a railroad. It was a network of people. The network helped enslaved people escape to freedom. Some "conductors" on the railroad led enslaved people by foot or wagon to safe places. Other people opened their homes and barns to give shelter. Some gave money, clothes, and food to help. Before the end of slavery in the United States, thousands of people used the Underground Railroad to escape slavery.

Even with all that help, the path to freedom was not easy. The trip often took weeks. It was very dangerous. Many of the people who used the railroad agreed that the long journey was a small price to pay for freedom.

Children read text closely to determine what the text says.

Name ______________________________

Look for Clues

Tell what the word *conductor* means in this text.

____

____

Look for Clues: Extend Your Ideas

Underline the meaning of *railroad* as used in the text.

Ask Questions

Write a question you have about the Underground Railroad.

____

____

Ask Questions: Extend Your Ideas

On a sheet of paper, write a question you might ask a "conductor" of the Underground Railroad.

Make Your Case

Circle words that help you understand how difficult it was to escape from slavery.

On a sheet of paper, write which hardship you think would be most difficult and why.

Make Your Case: Extend Your Ideas

On a sheet of paper, tell why the Underground Railroad was difficult for "conductors" as well as escaping slaves.

Children read text closely to determine what the text says.

Name ____________________

Writing

DIRECTIONS Write a paragraph about why you think it is important to live by example. Revisit *John Chapman: Planter and Pioneer* to find evidence that supports your opinion. Remember to introduce your topic in an interesting way, and to end your paragraph by summarizing your ideas.

Conventions

Apostrophes Circle the possessive nouns. Then write your own sentence that uses an apostrophe.

1. children's teacher's can't doctors' she'll

2.

Children write routinely for a range of tasks, purposes, and audiences. Children practice various conventions of standard English.

Benchmark Vocabulary

Name ______________________________

DIRECTIONS Write sentences using the words below.

clever planter tattered

Write in Response to Reading

DIRECTIONS Reread p. 19 of *John Chapman: Planter and Pioneer.* What reasons does the author provide to support the idea that John was a clever man? Use examples from the text to support your answer.

Children demonstrate contextual understanding of Benchmark Vocabulary. Children read text closely and use text evidence in their written answers.

Name ______________________

Reading Analysis

DIRECTIONS Using evidence from the text, answer the following questions about pp. 17–23 of *John Chapman: Planter and Pioneer.*

1. Reread p. 19. What reason does the author provide to support the idea that John worked hard?

2. Reread pp. 20–21. List four reasons the author provides to support the idea that John's home "was still the great outdoors."

Reason 1: ______________________

Reason 2: ______________________

Reason 3: ______________________

Reason 4: ______________________

3. Reread p. 22. Why did John sometimes get cold?

Children analyze and respond to literary and informational text.

Name ______________________

Writing

DIRECTIONS Reread pp. 17–23 of *John Chapman: Planter and Pioneer.* Write a paragraph that answers the following question: Was Johnny Appleseed a hero? Explain why or why not. Use linking words to connect your opinion and reasons. Revisit the text for examples to support your answer.

Conventions

Possessive Pronouns Write your own sentences that use two of the following possessive pronouns: *her, hers; their, theirs; our, ours.*

1. ______________________

2. ______________________

Children write routinely for a range of tasks, purposes, and audiences. Children practice various conventions of standard English.

Name ______________________________

Benchmark Vocabulary

DIRECTIONS Write sentences using the words below.

hero   creatures   legend

Write in Response to Reading

DIRECTIONS Reread p. 31 of *John Chapman: Planter and Pioneer.* How does the text on this page contribute to the author's purpose? Use evidence from the text to support your answer.

Children demonstrate contextual understanding of Benchmark Vocabulary. Children read text closely and use text evidence in their written answers.

Name ______________________

DIRECTIONS Using evidence from the text, answer the following questions about pp. 24–32 of *John Chapman: Planter and Pioneer.*

1. Reread p. 25. What is the meaning of the word *cubs*?

2. What could help you find out the meaning if you did not know it?

3. Reread p. 28. What is the meaning of the word *superman*?

4. What words or phrases does the author use to support the idea above?

Children analyze and respond to literary and informational text.

Name ____________________

Writing

DIRECTIONS Write a letter to a friend that gives your opinion about whether or not you believe one of the stories in the book *John Chapman: Planter and Pioneer.* Remember to tell your friend why you are writing to them. Revisit the text to find examples and details to support your opinion.

Conventions

Possessive Pronouns Write your own sentences that use two of the following possessive pronouns: *mine, hers, his, theirs, ours.*

1. ____________________

2. ____________________

Children write routinely for a range of tasks, purposes, and audiences. Children practice various conventions of standard English.

Name ______________________

Vowel Digraphs *oo, ue, ew, ui*

m**<u>oo</u>**n

gl**<u>ue</u>**

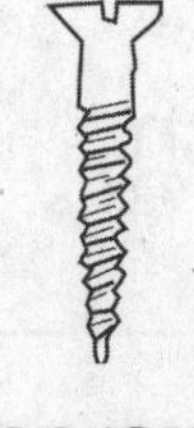
scr**<u>ew</u>**

fr**<u>ui</u>**t

Circle the word that has the same vowel sound as **moon**. **Write** the word on the line.

1. uncut untrue unplug ______________	2. grew grow grain ______________
3. stood spoon spun ______________	4. just joy juice ______________

Circle a word to finish each sentence. **Choose** a word that has the same vowel sound as **new**.

5. I ______ home from Roy's house on a plane.

   flow fun flew

6. I just unpacked my ______.

   sudden suitcase supper

7. I want to ______ the library book about cows.

   renew repeat recess

Children apply grade-level phonics and word analysis skills.

Name ______________________________

Benchmark Vocabulary

DIRECTIONS Write sentences using the words below.

stretch thankful

Write in Response to Reading

DIRECTIONS Revisit pp. 3–32 of *John Chapman: Planter and Pioneer*. Write about the part of Johnny Appleseed's life that you most admire. Use evidence from the text to support your answer.

Children demonstrate contextual understanding of Benchmark Vocabulary. Children read text closely and use text evidence in their written answers.

Writing

Name ______________________

DIRECTIONS Write an opinion about whether or not you think Johnny Appleseed's work made our world a better place. Remember to clearly state an opinion and support it with reasons. You should also provide a well-developed conclusion.

Conventions

Simple Sentences Write simple sentences using the given subjects and verbs below.

1. girl played

2. they walked

Children write routinely for a range of tasks, purposes, and audiences. Children practice various conventions of standard English.

Name ______________________

Benchmark Vocabulary

DIRECTIONS Write a sentence using the word below.

settlers

Write in Response to Reading

DIRECTIONS Revisit pp. 51–69 of *Johnny Appleseed.* What kinds of information would you add to the timeline? Explain why you would add this information. Use examples from the text to support your answer.

Children demonstrate contextual understanding of Benchmark Vocabulary. Children read text closely and use text evidence in their written answers.

Name ______________________________

DIRECTIONS Revisit pp. 64–65 of *Johnny Appleseed.* Which text feature in this section do you think is more informative – the timeline or the caption? Use evidence from the text to support your answer.

Children analyze and respond to literary and informational text.

Name ______________________

DIRECTIONS Write an opinion paragraph that states whether using the timeline helped you understand the text. State your opinion clearly and give reasons that support that opinion. Use linking words and phrases to connect ideas. Remember to include a concluding statement.

Expand Simple Sentences Add adjectives to the simple sentences below.

1. John wanted to see the frontier.

2. He liked to play in the woods.

Children write routinely for a range of tasks, purposes, and audiences. Children practice various conventions of standard English.

Benchmark Vocabulary

Name ______________________________

DIRECTIONS Write a sentence using the word below.

orchards

____

Write in Response to Reading

DIRECTIONS Reread pp. 56–57 of *Johnny Appleseed.* What text features does the author provide that help you locate facts? Use examples from the text to support your answer.

____

Children demonstrate contextual understanding of Benchmark Vocabulary. Children read text closely and use text evidence in their written answers.

Name ______________________

Writing

DIRECTIONS On a separate sheet of paper, write an opinion that states whether you would add headings to the text. Or, do you think the time line gives you enough information about what is on the page? Use linking words such as *and, because,* and *also* to connect your opinion and reasons. Remember to provide a concluding statement.

Conventions

Expand Simple Sentences Add an adverb to the simple sentences below.

1. He ______________ walked around the country planting apple trees.

2. John ______________ collected apple seeds from cider mills.

Children write routinely for a range of tasks, purposes, and audiences. Children practice various conventions of standard English.

Benchmark Vocabulary

Name ______________________________

DIRECTIONS Write a sentence using the word below.

nickname

Write in Response to Reading

DIRECTIONS Reread pp. 62–69 of *Johnny Appleseed.* How did Johnny Appleseed help settlers and the land? Do you think these reasons are strong enough to remember him so many years later? Use examples from the text to support your answer.

Children demonstrate contextual understanding of Benchmark Vocabulary. Children read text closely and use text evidence in their written answers.

Name ______________________________

DIRECTIONS The message on John Chapman's gravestone reads: *He lived for others.* Revisit the text and find three or four reasons that support the message on his gravestone. Write these reasons on the lines below. Use evidence from the text.

Children analyze and respond to literary and informational text.

Writing

Name ___________________________

DIRECTIONS Revisit p. 68 of *Johnny Appleseed* and reread the message on John Chapman's gravestone. Write an opinion statement about whether or not you agree with the message. If you agree, then explain why. If you do not, then tell what message you would put instead and why. Use linking words such as *because, and,* and *also* to connect opinions. Remember to provide a concluding statement.

Conventions

Expand Simple Sentences Combine the simple sentences below into one sentence with a compound subject. Then write your own sentence with a compound subject.

1. Marta planted flowers. Josie planted flowers.

2.

Children write routinely for a range of tasks, purposes, and audiences. Children practice various conventions of standard English.

Name ______________________________

Benchmark Vocabulary

DIRECTIONS Write a sentence using the word below.

frontier

Write in Response to Reading

DIRECTIONS Revisit pp. 62–63 of *Johnny Appleseed.* How does the information in this section support the text's main purpose? Use examples from the text to support your answer.

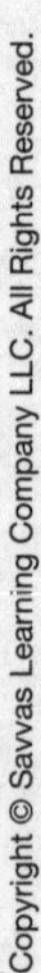

Children demonstrate contextual understanding of Benchmark Vocabulary. Children read text closely and use text evidence in their written answers.

Name ______________________________

DIRECTIONS Using evidence from the text, answer the following question about pp. 51–69 of *Johnny Appleseed.*

1. Think about the main purpose of *Johnny Appleseed.* Then write a paragraph about the text's main purpose and the details that support it. Use text evidence to support your opinion.

Children analyze and respond to literary and informational text.

Name ______________________________

Writing

DIRECTIONS You will write an opinion piece about which book you feel is more informative about John Chapman's life – *John Chapman: Planter and Pioneer* or *Johnny Appleseed.* Use the Venn diagram from Writing Workshop to make a list of points that you can use in your opinion piece. Then, on a separate sheet of paper, write an opinion statement about the text you think is more informative.

Conventions

Expand Simple Sentences Combine the simple sentences below into a single sentence with a compound verb. Then write your own sentence that uses a compound verb.

1. John gave apple seeds. John sold apple seeds.

2. ______________________________

Children write routinely for a range of tasks, purposes, and audiences. Children practice various conventions of standard English.

Name ______________________________

Suffixes *-ly, -ful, -er, -or, -ish*

teach + *er* = teach**er** sail + *or* = sail**or** child + *ish* = child**ish**

Add *-er, -or,* or ***-ish*** to each word to make a word.
Write the new word on the line.

visit

1. ______________

fool

2. ______________

sing

3. ______________

act

4. ______________

self

5. ______________

help

6. ______________

slow + *ly* = slow**ly** cheer + *ful* = cheer**ful**

Add *-ly* or ***-ful*** to each word to make a new word.
Write the new word on the line.

week

7. ______________

joy

8. ______________

quick

9. ______________

hope

10. ______________

Children apply grade-level phonics and word analysis skills.

Name ______________________________

Benchmark Vocabulary

DIRECTIONS Write sentences using the words below.

boughs drowsy

Write in Response to Reading

DIRECTIONS Reread "Planting a Tree" and "Trees" on pp. 118–119. Why would a poet repeat lines in a poem? Do you think repetition in a poem makes it better? Use examples from the text to support your answer.

Children demonstrate contextual understanding of Benchmark Vocabulary. Children read text closely and use text evidence in their written answers.

Name ______________________________

DIRECTIONS Revisit the list of points you would like to include in your opinion piece. On a separate sheet of paper, write a draft of your opinion about which book you feel is more informative about John Chapman's life – *John Chapman: Planter and Pioneer* or *Johnny Appleseed.* Remember to use linking words to connect your opinions and reasons.

Conventions

Rearrange Simple Sentences Rearrange the words in the simple sentences below.

1. In 1838, John moved to Indiana.

____

2. He was given the name Johnny Appleseed by settlers.

____

____

Children write routinely for a range of tasks, purposes, and audiences. Children practice various conventions of standard English.

Name ______________________

Benchmark Vocabulary

DIRECTIONS Write sentences using the words below.

wild hero

Write in Response to Reading

DIRECTIONS Which text do you like more – *John Chapman: Planter and Pioneer* or *Johnny Appleseed?* Explain why. Use evidence from the text to support your answer.

Children demonstrate contextual understanding of Benchmark Vocabulary. Children read text closely and use text evidence in their written answers.

Name ______________________

DIRECTIONS Write three ways that *John Chapman: Planter and Pioneer* and *Johnny Appleseed* are similar. Then explain how the texts are different. Use evidence from both texts to support your answer.

Children analyze and respond to literary and informational text.

Name ______________________

Writing

DIRECTIONS Think of ways to improve the draft of your opinion piece about the book you feel is more informative about John Chapman's life—*John Chapman: Planter and Pioneer* or *Johnny Appleseed.* Add linking words to make the connections between opinions, reasons, and ideas stronger. Rearrange sentences to add interest and variety. Include a concluding statement or section to wrap up your ideas. Revise your writing on a separate sheet of paper.

Conventions

Expand and Rearrange Sentences Rewrite the sentences below by rearranging and expanding them.

1. The other night we sat in our backyard. We watched falling stars. We saw about a dozen of them.

2. He walked along the country road. He stopped to plant apple trees. He stopped to speak with settlers.

Children write routinely for a range of tasks, purposes, and audiences. Children practice various conventions of standard English.

Benchmark Vocabulary

Name ______________________________

DIRECTIONS Write sentences using the words below.

planter orchards

Write in Response to Reading

DIRECTIONS Revisit *John Chapman: Planter and Pioneer* and *Johnny Appleseed.* Write several reasons why authors include different material when writing about the same topic. Use evidence from the text to support your answer.

Children demonstrate contextual understanding of Benchmark Vocabulary. Children read text closely and use text evidence in their written answers.

Name ______________________________

A Journey North

Harlem is a very interesting place. In the early 1900s many African Americans headed north. They left the South to find a new life in the North. Many settled in Harlem. Harlem is a neighborhood in New York City.

Life in the South had been hard. There were few jobs. The North had more jobs and the chance of a better life.

African Americans hoped they would get jobs in factories in the North. They dreamt of making more money. They wanted better schools for their children.

Most African Americans lived in the South. Their journey north changed that. More than half of all African Americans moved from the South. However, some had never lived in cities. Cities were big and noisy. It was difficult to live in a new place. Many found comfort living in neighborhoods with other African Americans.

Harlem became the largest African American neighborhood in the country. A group of artists, musicians, and singers used their talents to show African American culture. Palmer Hayden painted paintings of African Americans in the South and the North. Other artists sang songs or wrote about their experiences. They shared the journeys of African Americans with America.

Children read text closely to determine what the text says.

Name ______________________________

Look for Clues
Underline clues in the selection that tell why people moved to Harlem.

Look for Clues: Extend Your Ideas
Circle a reason why people moved from the South to the North.

Ask Questions
Write a question that you have about Harlem after reading this selection.

____

Ask Questions: Extend Your Ideas
Write a question to ask Palmer Hayden.

____

Make Your Case
Which piece of information in the selection makes Harlem seem most interesting to you?

____

Make Your Case: Extend Your Ideas
On a sheet of paper, write a headline for a newspaper article about Harlem.

____

Children read text closely to determine what the text says.

Name ______________________________

Writing

DIRECTIONS Use the Editing Checklist to edit your revised drafts. You may want to use different colored pencils to mark your corrections. Remember that you can use a dictionary to check the spelling of any words you are unsure of. On a separate sheet of paper, publish or print your final draft.

Conventions

Rearrange Simple and Compound Sentences Rewrite the sentences below by rearranging and expanding them.

We went to the apple orchard. I picked Red Delicious apples. My mom picked Golden Delicious apples. My brother went through the corn maze.

Children write routinely for a range of tasks, purposes, and audiences. Children practice various conventions of standard English.

Name ______________________________

Prefixes *un-, re-, pre-, dis-*

un + happy = **unhappy** *dis* + regard = **disregard**
re + paint = **repaint** *pre* + game = **pregame**

disagree	disloyal	disregard	reapply	prepay
preteen	replay	reread	unsafe	unlocked

Write words with ***un-, re-, pre-,*** or ***dis-*** to match each clue.

Use the words in the box if you need help.

1. play again ______	**2.** not agree ______
3. not regard ______	**4.** pay in advance ______
5. not locked ______	**6.** not loyal ______
7. not yet a teen ______	**8.** apply again ______
9. not safe ______	**10.** read again ______

Children apply grade-level phonics and word analysis skills.

Name ______________________

Benchmark Vocabulary

DIRECTIONS Write sentences using the words below.

conflict   fortune

Write in Response to Reading

DIRECTIONS Reread pp. 1–9 of *Pioneers to the West*. Why do you think the author used different types of paper for different text feature boxes throughout the book? Use evidence from the text to support your answer.

Children demonstrate contextual understanding of Benchmark Vocabulary. Children read text closely and use text evidence in their written answers.

Writing

Name ______________________

DIRECTIONS Think about what you have read in *Pioneers to the West.* Then make connections between the title of the text and the title of the unit—Pioneering New Ideas and New Worlds. Write a story in which you are a pioneer traveling across the country in search of a new opportunity. Use facts and details from the text to support your story.

Conventions

Use Simple Sentences Underline the subject in each sentence.

1. The family moved west on a covered wagon.
2. George Staples was born in England.

Children write routinely for a range of tasks, purposes, and audiences. Children practice various conventions of standard English.

Name ______________________

Benchmark Vocabulary

DIRECTIONS Write sentences using the words below.

bound typical

Write in Response to Reading

DIRECTIONS Reread pp. 10–11 of *Pioneers to the West*. What caused so many people to flock to California in 1849? Use evidence from the text to support your answer.

Children demonstrate contextual understanding of Benchmark Vocabulary. Children read text closely and use text evidence in their written answers.

Name ______________________________

DIRECTIONS Using evidence from the text, answer the following question about pp. 10–13 of *Pioneers to the West*.

1. Reread pp. 10–13. Select an event that happened and reasons for why that event happened. Write a few sentences that explain what happened and why. Remember to use signal words such as *because* to help you explain why the event happened.

Children analyze and respond to literary and informational text.

Name ______________________

Writing

DIRECTIONS Think about what you read in *Pioneers to the West* about the life of John McWilliams, and the most important events that happened to him. How might the chart you worked on help you to write a narrative about John McWilliams?

Conventions

Prepositional Phrases Underline the prepositional phrase in the sentence below. Then write your own sentence that uses a prepositional phrase.

1. The inspector found gold at the sawmill.

2. ______________________

Children write routinely for a range of tasks, purposes, and audiences. Children practice various conventions of standard English.

Benchmark Vocabulary

Name ______________________________

DIRECTIONS Write sentences using the words below.

territory opportunities

Write in Response to Reading

DIRECTIONS Reread pp. 14–19 of *Pioneers to the West*. How does asking and answering questions help you understand what you read? Use evidence from the text to support your answer.

Children demonstrate contextual understanding of Benchmark Vocabulary. Children read text closely and use text evidence in their written answers.

Name ______________________

DIRECTIONS Using evidence from the text, answer the following questions about pp. 14–19 of *Pioneers to the West*.

1. What is a temporal word?

2. Reread the first paragraph on p. 16. What temporal word is used?

3. Reread the first paragraph on p. 17. What temporal word is used?

4. How do the temporal words help you understand what is happening in this section?

Children analyze and respond to literary and informational text.

Writing

Name ______________________

DIRECTIONS Consider what you read about Laura Ingalls Wilder in *Pioneers to the West*. Use a Story Sequence Chart to help you plan a narrative about her childhood. Identify the characters and setting of your narrative. Then write several sentences about how the planning chart will help you write your narrative.

Conventions

Prepositional Phrases Underline the prepositional phrases that tell **when** something happened.

On Wednesday, Patty and Maddie looked out the window. Rain fell. In April, it had rained a lot. The girls wanted to play before it rained again.

Children write routinely for a range of tasks, purposes, and audiences. Children practice various conventions of standard English.

Name ______________________

Benchmark Vocabulary

DIRECTIONS Write a sentence using the word below.

blizzard

Write in Response to Reading

DIRECTIONS Do you think the advertisement on p. 20 of *Pioneers to the West* would convince your family to move west? Use evidence from the text to support your answer.

Children demonstrate contextual understanding of Benchmark Vocabulary. Children read text closely and use text evidence in their written answers.

Name ______________________

DIRECTIONS Look at the photograph on p. 23 of *Pioneers to the West*. Write the main idea of this photograph. Then write the key details that are found in the photo's caption.

Main Idea:

Key Details:

Children analyze and respond to literary and informational text.

Name ______________________________

Writing

DIRECTIONS On a separate sheet of paper, write the first draft of your narrative about Laura Ingalls Wilder. Your narrative should follow the events outlined on your Story Sequence Chart. Include details about Laura's thoughts, feelings, words, and actions to help readers understand Laura's character better. Return to the text to gather facts about Laura's childhood.

Conventions

Prepositional Phrases Add a prepositional phrase to the sentence below. Then write your own sentences that use prepositional phrases.

1. Ruth Chrisman saved her students ______________________________

2. ______________________________

3. ______________________________

Children write routinely for a range of tasks, purposes, and audiences. Children practice various conventions of standard English.

Benchmark Vocabulary

Name ______________________

DIRECTIONS Write sentences using the words below.

destiny   progress

Write in Response to Reading

DIRECTIONS Reread pp. 26–29 of *Pioneers to the West*. Explain a connection between two historical events discussed in this section. Use evidence from the text to support your answer.

Children demonstrate contextual understanding of Benchmark Vocabulary. Children read text closely and use text evidence in their written answers.

Name ______________________

Reading Analysis

DIRECTIONS Reread pp. 26–27 of *Pioneers to the West*. Write a paragraph that describes the connection between Manifest Destiny and the Trail of Tears. Use evidence from the text to support your answer.

Children analyze and respond to literary and informational text.

Name ______________________

Writing

DIRECTIONS Identify and describe a connection between the Homestead Act and another event in *Pioneers to the West*.

Conventions

Prepositional Phrases Expand the simple sentences below by adding prepositional phrases.

1. A person just had to be 21 years old.

2. Ruth started teaching school.

Children write routinely for a range of tasks, purposes, and audiences. Children practice various conventions of standard English.

Name ______________________

Phonics

Consonant Patterns *kn, wr, gn, mb*

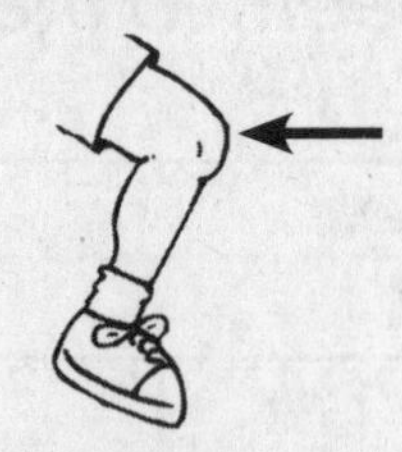

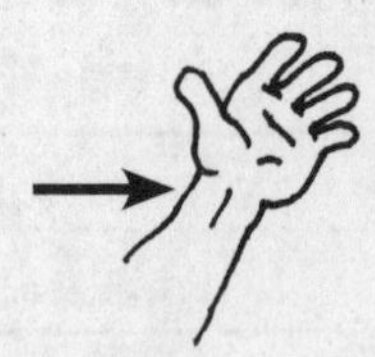

knee　　**wr**ist　　si**gn**　　la**mb**

Say the word for each picture.
Write kn, wr, gn, or **mb** to finish each word.

1. 
____ench

2. co____

3. 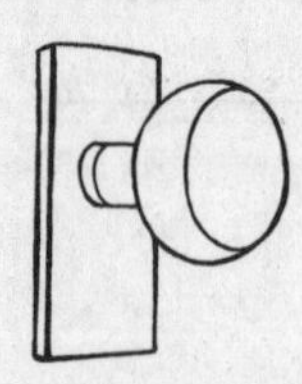
____ob

4. 
____at

5. 
cli____

6. 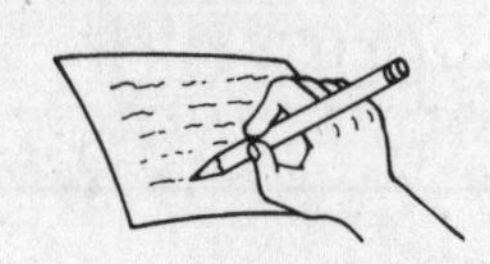
____ite

7. 
____ock

8. 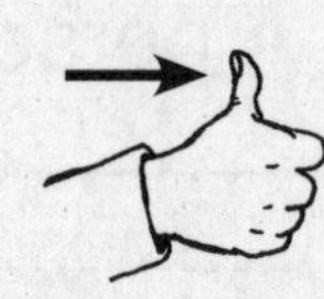
thu____

Find the word that has the same beginning sound as the picture.

Mark the space to show your answer.

9. ❑ wrong
❑ wing
❑ white

10. ❑ king
❑ knife
❑ kick

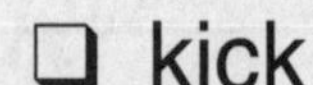

Children apply grade-level phonics and word analysis skills.

Name ________________________

Benchmark Vocabulary

DIRECTIONS Write a sentence using the word below.

advertisements

Write in Response to Reading

DIRECTIONS Reread pp. 4–5 and 26–29 of *Pioneers of the West*. Select one of the images and tell what you learned from it. How does it contribute to the text? Use evidence from the text to support your answer.

Children demonstrate contextual understanding of Benchmark Vocabulary. Children read text closely and use text evidence in their written answers.

Name ____________________

Writing

DIRECTIONS Return to your Laura Ingalls Wilder narrative. Plan some illustrations that you want to include with your narrative, noting why each one would be useful to the reader. List the main event of your narrative and the kinds of illustrations you want to include. Then write a short description and caption for each illustration. Write your plan on a separate sheet of paper.

Conventions

Rearrange Simple Sentences Rewrite the sentences below in a new way.

1. The pioneers found gold in California.

2. But this destiny came at a price.

3. Those who refused to leave faced the force of the U.S. Army.

Children write routinely for a range of tasks, purposes, and audiences. Children practice various conventions of standard English.

Benchmark Vocabulary

Name ______________________________

DIRECTIONS Write a sentence using the word below.

swaying

Write in Response to Reading

DIRECTIONS Reread p. 75 of *Going West*. Whose point of view do you most agree with – Mama's or Papa's? Why? Use examples from the text to support your answer.

Children demonstrate contextual understanding of Benchmark Vocabulary. Children read text closely and use text evidence in their written answers.

Name ______________________

DIRECTIONS Reread pp. 71–85. Choose two characters and identify the challenges they faced. Then explain how each character responded to those challenges. Use evidence from the text.

Children analyze and respond to literary and informational text.

Writing

Name ______________________

DIRECTIONS Revisit pp. 71–85 in *Going West*. Flag evidence in the text that helps you understand Mama's or Jake's point of view about the journey west. On a separate sheet of paper, write a statement that summarizes Mama's or Jake's point of view. Then write a new beginning from Mama's or Jake's point of view on the lines below.

Conventions

Rearrange Simple Sentences Rewrite the sentence below in a new way.

1. We were all tired of the rocking wagon and the dust.

Children write routinely for a range of tasks, purposes, and audiences. Children practice various conventions of standard English.

Name ______________________

Benchmark Vocabulary

DIRECTIONS Write sentences using the words below.

baking shriveling squashed

Write in Response to Reading

DIRECTIONS Reread pp. 96–98 of *Going West*. How do the details in this section support the central message of the text? Use details from the text to support your answer.

Children demonstrate contextual understanding of Benchmark Vocabulary. Children read text closely and use text evidence in their written answers.

Name ______________________________

From Seed to Flower to Fruit

Do you know where apples come from? Have you ever seen an apple **seed**? Inside that tiny brown shell is the beginning of a whole new tree.

Every seed contains an **embryo**, or a baby plant. The seed protects the baby plant. Then when the seed gets the right amount of water and warmth, it breaks open. The embryo begins to grow.

A **stem** with little seed **leaves** pushes upward. There may be one leaf or two leaves. The **seedling** wants light to help it grow. **Roots** also begin to grow. They help the seedling get the food from the soil.

New leaves grow from the stem. When there are enough new leaves, the seed leaves fall off. Soon, **flower buds** appear. When the flowers open, bees move pollen from one flower to another. New seeds form inside the flower.

The part of the plant where these seeds are grows larger. It becomes a tiny **apple**, and soon it will be ready to eat. Do you see the seeds inside? Each seed is ready for a chance to become a new plant. The cycle begins again!

Children read text closely to determine what the text says.

Name ______________________

Look for Clues

Turn to a partner and tell why some words are in bolder print and how that helps you as you read.

Look for Clues: Extend Your Ideas

Using clues from the text, tell a partner what the word *seed* means.

____

____

Ask Questions

Write a question that you would ask a gardener if you planned on growing an apple tree.

____

____

Make Your Case

On a sheet of paper, draw an apple tree and label it. Then write which part of the growing process you think is most interesting.

Make Your Case: Extend Your Ideas

In the article, underline the terms that you should include in your picture.

Children read text closely to determine what the text says.

Name ______________________

Writing

DIRECTIONS Revisit the class's narrative scene and consider where the writing might change in order to write the scene from Mama's or Papa's point of view. Then rewrite the scene from the point of view of Mama or Papa.

Conventions

Combining Sentences Combine the simple sentences below into compound sentences.

1. Sam set the table. Mom cooked dinner.

2. The storm was over. The crops were smashed.

Children write routinely for a range of tasks, purposes, and audiences.
Children practice various conventions of standard English.

Name ______________________

Benchmark Vocabulary

DIRECTIONS Write sentences using the words below.

stable   howling

Write in Response to Reading

DIRECTIONS Reread p. 107 of *Going West*. What kind of weather is the family experiencing? Use specific details and evidence from the text to support your answer.

Children demonstrate contextual understanding of Benchmark Vocabulary. Children read text closely and use text evidence in their written answers.

Name ______________________

DIRECTIONS Using evidence from the text, answer the following question about pp. 100–117 of *Going West*.

1. Reread p. 117. Write a paragraph that tells how the events of the beginning and middle of the story affect how you feel about the ending. Use examples from the text to support your answer.

Children analyze and respond to literary and informational text.

Name ______________________________

Writing

DIRECTIONS Write a narrative about a child who wants to be a pioneer. Your narrative should have a beginning, middle, and end. Include at least three prepositional phrases and specific details that describe characters and events.

Conventions

Prepositional Phrases Write a sentence using one of the prepositions below.

through in on under above

Children write routinely for a range of tasks, purposes, and audiences. Children practice various conventions of standard English.

Benchmark Vocabulary

Name ______________________

DIRECTIONS Write sentences using the words below.

constant mounds

Write in Response to Reading

DIRECTIONS Revisit *Going West*. Why is it important for people living today to understand the life of pioneers? How does this relate to the central message of the text? Use evidence from the text to explain your thoughts.

Children demonstrate contextual understanding of Benchmark Vocabulary. Children read text closely and use text evidence in their written answers.

Name ______________________

DIRECTIONS Reread pp. 116–117 of *Going West*. Tell what the central message of the text is. Then explain how the story's conclusion contributes to the central message. Use details and evidence from the text to support your answer.

Children analyze and respond to literary and informational text.

Writing

Name ______________________

DIRECTIONS Revise your narrative from the previous lesson.

Conventions

Expand Sentences Expand the sentence by adding adjectives or adverbs to it.

1. The children ran to see the piglets.

Children write routinely for a range of tasks, purposes, and audiences. Children practice various conventions of standard English.

Name ____________________

Phonics

Consonant Patterns *ph, gh, ck, ng*

phone

cou**gh**

clo**ck**

ri**ng**

backpack	elephant	laughter	trophy	
ticket	hanger	graph	photo	dolphin

Pick a word from the box to match each clue.
Write the word on the line.

1.  ____________________

2.  ____________________

3.  ____________________

4. 

____

5.  ____________________

6.  ____________________

Pick a word from the box above to finish each sentence.
Write the word on the line.

7. Roy wears a ____________________.

8. Sue is taking a ____________________ of Roy.

Children apply grade-level phonics and word analysis skills.

Benchmark Vocabulary

Name ___________________________

DIRECTIONS Write sentences using the words below.

territory destiny

Write in Response to Reading

DIRECTIONS Which text do you like more—*Pioneers to the West* or *Going West*? Explain why. Use evidence from the text to support your answer.

Children demonstrate contextual understanding of Benchmark Vocabulary. Children read text closely and use text evidence in their written answers.

Name ______________________

Writing

DIRECTIONS Write a first draft of your pioneer narrative. Remember that it is fine to change things in the Story Sequence Map or Character Web if you have new ideas while you write. Use details to describe characters' thoughts, actions, and feelings.

Conventions

Rearrange Sentences Write two more interesting sentences about the family's vacation.

1. ______________________

2. ______________________

Children write routinely for a range of tasks, purposes, and audiences. Children practice various conventions of standard English.

Benchmark Vocabulary

Name ______________________

DIRECTIONS Write a sentence using the word below.

progress

Write in Response to Reading

DIRECTIONS What kind of text do you most like to read—informational or narrative? Use evidence from *Pioneers to the West* and *Going West* to support your answer.

Children demonstrate contextual understanding of Benchmark Vocabulary. Children read text closely and use text evidence in their written answers.

Name ______________________________

DIRECTIONS In which text do you find the images most helpful – *Pioneers to the West* or *Going West?* Explain why. Use evidence from both texts to support your answer.

Children analyze and respond to literary and informational text.

Writing

Name ______________________

DIRECTIONS Revise the narrative you have been working on. Reread your narrative multiple times—checking for mistakes in spelling, punctuation, and capitalization.

Conventions

Rearrange Sentences Write three sentences that tell a sequence of events out of order. Then exchange sentences with a partner and rearrange his or her sentences.

Children write routinely for a range of tasks, purposes, and audiences. Children practice various conventions of standard English.

Name ______________________

Vowel Patterns *aw, au, augh, al*

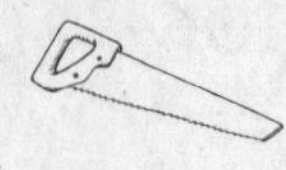   

s**aw** **au**to c**augh**t ch**al**k

Write a word from the box to match each picture.

daughter	draw	fall	naughty	raw	sauce	thaw	walk

1. ______________

2. 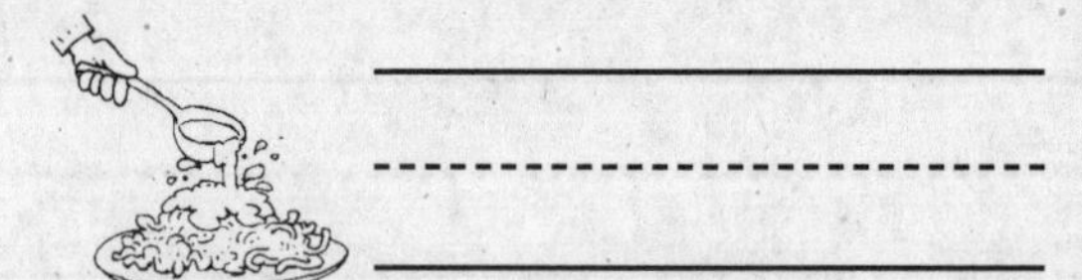 ______________

3.  ______________

4. 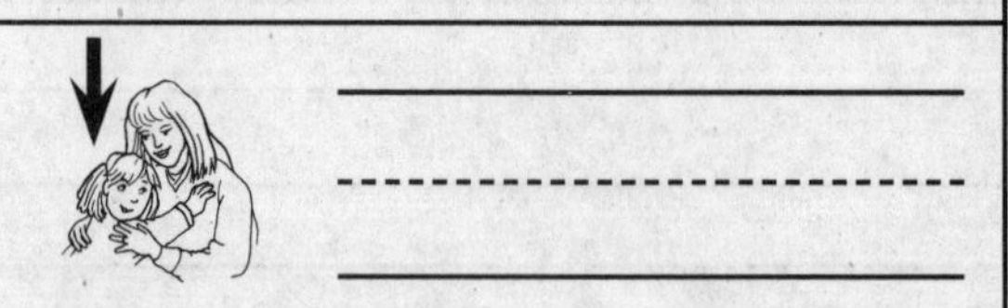 ______________

Write a word from the box that is the opposite of each word below.

freeze

5. ______________

rise

6. ______________

good

7. ______________

cooked

8. ______________

Mark the space next to the word that has the same vowel sound as *saw.*

9. ☐ fault
   ☐ find
   ☐ few

10. ☐ tray
    ☐ took
    ☐ taught

 Children apply grade-level phonics and word analysis skills.

Benchmark Vocabulary

Name ______________________________

DIRECTIONS Write sentences using the words below.

reflected resources

Write in Response to Reading

DIRECTIONS What is the main idea of the second paragraph on p. 3 of *68 Ways to Save the Planet Before Bedtime?* How does it relate to the main topic of the text? Use evidence from the text to support your answer.

Children demonstrate contextual understanding of Benchmark Vocabulary. Children read text closely and use text evidence in their written answers.

Name ______________________

Writing

DIRECTIONS Revisit the main topics and key details discussed during the lesson. Choose one main topic and key details that you felt were most interesting. Create a chart to help you plan your writing. Then, on a separate sheet of paper, write an opinion about why you thought those key details supported the main topic, and why you found them interesting.

Conventions

Consonant Digraphs Circle the consonant digraphs. Then write a sentence that uses two of the words below.

1. teacher graph think when

2. ______________________

Children write routinely for a range of tasks, purposes, and audiences. Children practice various conventions of standard English.

Name ______________________

Benchmark Vocabulary

DIRECTIONS Write sentences using the words below.

dangerous litter waste

Write in Response to Reading

DIRECTIONS Reread p. 4 of *68 Ways to Save the Planet Before Bedtime*. How does the graphic on this page help you understand spiders? Use examples from the text to support your answer.

Children demonstrate contextual understanding of Benchmark Vocabulary. Children read text closely and use text evidence in their written answers.

Name ______________________________

DIRECTIONS Revisit pp. 4–7 of *68 Ways to Save the Planet Before Bedtime.* Select two text features and explain how each one adds to your understanding of the text. Use evidence from the text to support your answer.

Children analyze and respond to literary and informational text.

Name ______________________

Writing

DIRECTIONS Think about how *68 Ways to Save the Planet Before Bedtime* connects with the theme and title of the unit, Changing the World. Flag text evidence that shows how the tips in the text can help change the world. Create a Main Purpose Chart to organize your thoughts. Then write a paragraph that explains the connection between the unit title and the text.

Conventions

Spelling Patterns – Vowel Digraphs Write two words for each vowel digraph.

1. ea- ______________________

2. ee- ______________________

Children write routinely for a range of tasks, purposes, and audiences. Children practice various conventions of standard English.

Name ______________________________

Benchmark Vocabulary

DIRECTIONS Write sentences using the words below.

impossible   persuade   switch   completely

Write in Response to Reading

DIRECTIONS Reread pp. 8–11 of *68 Ways to Save the Planet Before Bedtime.* What's one connection between global warming and conserving electricity? Use evidence from the text to support your answer.

Children demonstrate contextual understanding of Benchmark Vocabulary. Children read text closely and use text evidence in their written answers.

Name ______________________________

Picking Up Sunset Park

Lacey stood at the gate of Sunset Park. What she saw made her want to cry. The storm had knocked down two small trees and scattered branches everywhere.

Her brother, Jared, looked at the mess. "We might as well go home," he said. "It's going to be a while before we can play here again."

"Let's pick up some of the branches," Lacey said.

"That will take all day!" Jared said.

"If we work together, we can get it done quickly," Lacey said.

They began to pick up branches and pile them near the gate. As the pile grew, their friends Marius and Elsa rode by.

"What's going on?" Marius asked.

"The storm blew down some trees," Lacey said. "We're cleaning up."

Marius and Elsa hopped off their bikes and began working. Soon, some neighbors saw the kids at work. They started to help clean up too. Mrs. Cleary came with cold lemonade for everyone. Before long, the branches were all cleared. The adults cut the fallen trees and moved them to the side. The park was almost as good as new. Lacey and Jared happily ran to the swings. They were thrilled. There was even time to play before dinner!

Children read text closely to determine what the text says.

Name ______________________________

Sleuth Work

Look for Clues
Underline clues in the story that tell how bad the storm damage was.

Look for Clues: Extend Your Ideas
Circle one way the characters picked up the park.

Ask Questions
Write a question you would ask one of the neighbors who stopped to help.

____

Ask Questions: Extend Your Ideas
You are a local newspaper reporter. Write a question you would ask Lacey.

____

Make Your Case
On a sheet of paper, tell what the writer wanted to explain. Explain, using examples from the text.

Make Your Case: Extend Your Ideas
Tell a partner three words you would use to describe Lacey and why.

Children read text closely to determine what the text says.

Writing

Name ______________________________

DIRECTIONS Reread tip 25 on p. 11 of *68 Ways to Save the Planet Before Bedtime*. Then write an opinion paragraph that tells whether or not you agree with the tip. Use a T-chart to list your reasons.

Conventions

Spelling Patterns – /g/ or /j/ Cross out the words that do not belong.

1. /g/: biology wagon garden

2. /j/: orange gentle flag

Children write routinely for a range of tasks, purposes, and audiences. Children practice various conventions of standard English.

Name ________________________

Benchmark Vocabulary

DIRECTIONS Write sentences using the words below.

reduce produce reuse

Write in Response to Reading

DIRECTIONS Reread p. 12 of *68 Ways to Save the Planet Before Bedtime*. How do the images on this page help to clarify the text? Use specific details and examples to support your answer.

Children demonstrate contextual understanding of Benchmark Vocabulary. Children read text closely and use text evidence in their written answers.

Name ______________________________

DIRECTIONS Reread pp. 14–15. The photographs in this section are meant to help you visualize the sequence for creating a sock monster. Is there anything that you would change or add to this section to improve the explanation? Explain why or why not. Use evidence from the text to support your answer.

Children analyze and respond to literary and informational text.

Name ______________________

Writing

DIRECTIONS Write an opinion paragraph about whether or not you think tips 39–44 on p. 15 of *68 Ways to Save the Planet Before Bedtime* are good ideas. Use linking words to connect your opinions and reasons.

Conventions

Spelling Patterns – Diphthongs *oi* and *oy* Write two *oi* words and two *oy* words.

1. *oi:* ______________________

2. *oy:* ______________________

Children write routinely for a range of tasks, purposes, and audiences. Children practice various conventions of standard English.

Benchmark Vocabulary

Name ________________

DIRECTIONS Write sentences using the words below.

reason passenger packaging

Write in Response to Reading

DIRECTIONS Reread pp. 16–17 of *68 Ways to Save the Planet Before Bedtime*. Do you think riding a bike is better for the environment than riding in a car? Use evidence from the text to support your answer.

Children demonstrate contextual understanding of Benchmark Vocabulary. Children read text closely and use text evidence in their written answers.

Name ______________________

DIRECTIONS Using evidence from the text, answer the following questions about pp. 16–19 of *68 Ways to Save the Planet Before Bedtime*.

1. Reread p. 16. What is one benefit of riding a bike?

2. Reread p. 18. How does using a library contribute to fewer books being made?

3. Why do you think recycling still contributes to pollution? Use examples from the text to support your answer.

Children analyze and respond to literary and informational text.

Name ______________________

Writing

DIRECTIONS Review tips 1–58 in *68 Ways to Save the Planet Before Bedtime*. Select two tips that you think are most important for saving the planet, and explain why. Remember to give reasons that support your opinion. Use linking words to connect your opinions and reasons.

Conventions

Spelling Patterns – Silent *gh* Underline the silent *gh* words. Then write one sentence that uses a silent *gh* word.

1. We caught a fish.
2. The cat climbed high.
3. ______________________

Children write routinely for a range of tasks, purposes, and audiences. Children practice various conventions of standard English.

Name ___________________________

Phonics

Inflected Endings *-s, -ed, -ing, -er, -est*

Read each word.
Find the base word.
Write the base word on the line.

try + *-s* = tr**ies** try + *-ed* = tr**ied** try + *-ing* = try**ing**

1. hiked ________	**2.** skipped ________
3. planning ________	**4.** shopping ________
5. cried ________	**6.** liking ________
7. baking ________	**8.** boxes ________

Find the word that makes sense in the sentences below.
Mark the space to show your answer.

9. Sam is _____ than Luke.

- ☐ fast
- ☐ faster
- ☐ fasting

10. Mia is the _____ person I know.

- ☐ kinder
- ☐ kind
- ☐ kindest

Children apply grade-level phonics and word analysis skills.

Benchmark Vocabulary

Name ______________________________

DIRECTIONS Write sentences using the words below.

selfish   sponsored   monitor   dragging

Write in Response to Reading

DIRECTIONS Reread p. 22 of *68 Ways to Save the Planet Before Bedtime*. How does the story on this page connect with the main purpose of the text? Use evidence from the text to support your answer.

Children demonstrate contextual understanding of Benchmark Vocabulary. Children read text closely and use text evidence in their written answers.

Name ______________________________

Writing

DIRECTIONS On a separate sheet of paper, list three tips from the book that you would want to share with your friends and family. Be sure to include the title and writer of the book. Then state an opinion about whether or not you thought the book was helpful. Remember to support your opinion with reasons, and to wrap it up with a strong conclusion.

Conventions

Compound Words Underline the compound word in each sentence. Then write your own sentence using a compound word. Underline the compound word.

1. The firefighter rescued the cat from the tree.
2. She used a flashlight when the lights went out.
3. ______________________________

Children write routinely for a range of tasks, purposes, and audiences. Children practice various conventions of standard English.

Benchmark Vocabulary

Name ______________________

DIRECTIONS Write a sentence using the word below.

pleaded

Write in Response to Reading

DIRECTIONS Reread pp. 4–7 of *On Meadowview Street*. What do you learn about Caroline's character in this section? Use details and examples from the text to support your answer.

Children demonstrate contextual understanding of Benchmark Vocabulary. Children read text closely and use text evidence in their written answers.

Name ______________________

Reading Analysis

DIRECTIONS Using evidence from the text, answer the following questions about *On Meadowview Street.*

1. Reread p. 6. What does the response of Caroline's dad tell you about his character?

2. Reread pp. 14–15. How do Caroline's parents respond when she tells them that her garden needs a shady spot?

3. Write several sentences about whether or not you admire Caroline and her parents. Do you think most people would take the time to create a meadow in their yard? Use specific examples and details from the text to support your answer.

Children analyze and respond to literary and informational text.

Writing

Name ______________________

DIRECTIONS Revisit *On Meadowview Street* and flag text evidence that helps you understand how Caroline inspired her family, and how her family inspired their neighbors to make changes. Then write an opinion paragraph about how Caroline and her family inspired others. Use linking words to connect opinions and reasons.

Conventions

Compound Words Circle the compound words. Then write your own sentence that uses a compound word.

1. sunflower neighbor playground lighthouse flying

2.

Children write routinely for a range of tasks, purposes, and audiences. Children practice various conventions of standard English.

Name ______________________________

Benchmark Vocabulary

DIRECTIONS Write a sentence using the word below.

unpacked

Write in Response to Reading

DIRECTIONS Reread pp. 6–7 of *On Meadowview Street.* How do the words *pleaded* and *raced* affect the story? Use examples from the text to support your answer.

Children demonstrate contextual understanding of Benchmark Vocabulary. Children read text closely and use text evidence in their written answers.

Name ________________________________

DIRECTIONS Reread pp. 1–13 of *On Meadowview Street.* Write a paragraph about the word choices the author makes. Use examples from the text to show how the author's word choices help you to understand the characters' thoughts, feelings, and actions.

Children analyze and respond to literary and informational text.

Name ____________________

Writing

DIRECTIONS Revisit *On Meadowview Street*. Then plan and write a short review that expresses your opinion about the story. Introduce the book, state an opinion about the story, and then support your opinion with reasons. Remember to provide a concluding statement.

Conventions

Prefixes Write two sentences that use the prefix *un-*.

1. ____________________

2. ____________________

Children write routinely for a range of tasks, purposes, and audiences. Children practice various conventions of standard English.

Benchmark Vocabulary

Name ______________________

DIRECTIONS Write a sentence using the word below.

zipping

____

____

____

Write in Response to Reading

DIRECTIONS Revisit pp. 14–21 of *On Meadowview Street*. Choose one illustration and explain what you learned from it. Use details from the text to support your answer.

____

____

____

____

____

____

Children demonstrate contextual understanding of Benchmark Vocabulary. Children read text closely and use text evidence in their written answers.

Name ______________________

Writing

DIRECTIONS Think of ways to make your review of *On Meadowview Street* stronger. Then revise and edit your review on a separate sheet of paper. Look for places to add powerful words, and make sure that your ideas are grouped logically. Add linking words to make the connections between opinions and reasons stronger.

Conventions

Prefixes Write two of your own sentences that use the prefix *re-*.

1. ______________________

2. ______________________

Children write routinely for a range of tasks, purposes, and audiences. Children practice various conventions of standard English.

Benchmark Vocabulary

Name ______________________________

DIRECTIONS Write a sentence using the word below.

shallow

Write in Response to Reading

DIRECTIONS Revisit pp. 28–29 of *On Meadowview Street*. How is the structure of this section different from the rest of the text? How does this add to the text? Use examples from the text to support your answer.

Children demonstrate contextual understanding of Benchmark Vocabulary. Children read text closely and use text evidence in their written answers.

Name ____________________

DIRECTIONS Revisit pp. 22–31 of *On Meadowview Street*. Write a paragraph that explains how events in the story are directly supported by illustrations. Do you like this type of story structure? Use specific details and examples from the text to support your answer.

Children analyze and respond to literary and informational text.

Writing

Name ______________________

DIRECTIONS Write a paragraph that identifies your opinion about why it is important to take care of Earth. Clearly state your opinion, and list reasons to support that opinion.

Conventions

Root Words Write the root word for each underlined word.

1. I want to be a <u>singer</u>. ____________

2. My sister is an <u>artist</u>. ____________

Children write routinely for a range of tasks, purposes, and audiences. Children practice various conventions of standard English.

Name ______________________________

Phonics

Abbreviations

Read each abbreviation.
Draw a line to the word it stands for.

1. Ave.	Doctor
2. Dr.	November
3. Mr.	Mister
4. Mon.	Avenue
5. Nov.	Street
6. St.	Monday

Write each abbreviation correctly.

7. apr ______________ **8.** mrs ______________

9. Mar ______________ **10.** fri ______________

Children apply grade-level phonics and word analysis skills.

Benchmark Vocabulary

Name ______________________________

DIRECTIONS Write sentences using the words below.

hunters pebble

Write in Response to Reading

DIRECTIONS Reread "The Lion and the Mouse" and "The Crow and the Pitcher." What is the central message of each fable? Which message do you like most? Use examples to support your answer.

Children demonstrate contextual understanding of Benchmark Vocabulary. Children read text closely and use text evidence in their written answers.

Name ______________________________

Writing

DIRECTIONS Revisit the plan you wrote for your opinion piece about why it is important for people to take care of Earth. Use your plan to draft your opinion piece on a separate sheet of paper. Remember to provide reasons and details that support your opinion. Arrange your reasons and supporting details in a logical order. Use linking words to connect opinions and reasons.

Conventions

Shades of Meaning Number the words from weakest (1) to strongest (3) in meaning. Then write your own sentence that uses a word with a similar meaning as the word *happy*.

1. freezing _____ cool _____ cold _____

2. angry _____ furious _____ mad _____

3. ______________________________

Children write routinely for a range of tasks, purposes, and audiences. Children practice various conventions of standard English.

Benchmark Vocabulary

Name ______________________

DIRECTIONS Write sentences using the words below.

resources persuade

Write in Response to Reading

DIRECTIONS Reread pp. 20–21 of *68 Ways to Save the Planet Before Bedtime*. What is one possible connection between the Fast Fact on p. 20 and the main topic of the text? Use examples from the text to support your answer.

Children demonstrate contextual understanding of Benchmark Vocabulary. Children read text closely and use text evidence in their written answers.

Name ______________________

DIRECTIONS Reread pp. 16–19 of *68 Ways to Save the Planet Before Bedtime*. How does the author use text features to connect concepts in this section? Use specific details and examples from pp. 16–19 to support your answer.

Children analyze and respond to literary and informational text.

Name ______________________________

DIRECTIONS Think of ways to revise your opinion piece from the previous lesson. Add reasons and examples to support your opinions. Add linking words to make stronger connections between opinions, reasons, and ideas. Write your revised opinion piece on a separate sheet of paper.

Shades of Meaning Circle one of the words below. Then write two words that have a similar meaning.

1. happy sad funny said

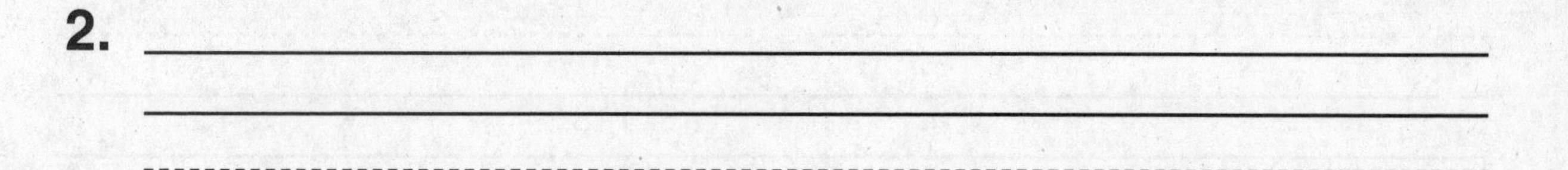

2. ______________________________

Children write routinely for a range of tasks, purposes, and audiences. Children practice various conventions of standard English.

Name ______________________________

Benchmark Vocabulary

DIRECTIONS Write sentences using the words below.

produce   pleaded

Write in Response to Reading

DIRECTIONS Revisit *68 Ways to Save the Planet Before Bedtime* and *On Meadowview Street*. In what ways are these two texts alike? In what ways are they different? Use examples from both texts to support your answer.

Children demonstrate contextual understanding of Benchmark Vocabulary. Children read text closely and use text evidence in their written answers.

Name ______________________________

Making a Difference, One Bag at a Time

When Annie Wignall was eleven, her mother told her something that made her sad. She said that some children have to leave their homes in hard times. They often must leave everything behind. They lose many things that they love and need. Annie wanted to do something to help. Annie made cute cloth bags for children in need. She found people to donate new items that children might miss from their homes. Annie filled the bags with these things. She put in soap and toothpaste. She found toys to add. She got games and books for the bags. She hoped to give these children lots to make them happy.

Annie started Care Bags Foundation. Every month Annie and other helpers prepare about one hundred Care Bags for Kids. Some people sew the bags. Others give things to put in the bags. Volunteers help fill them. The bags are then given to children in need. They bring many smiles! Care Bags Foundation also helps children in another way. It teaches kids how to make a difference. It tells how to start a Care Bags project in their own towns. Care Bags Foundation has made a big difference with each small bag!

Children read text closely to determine what the text says.

Name ______________________

Sleuth Work

Look for Clues

Underline clues. Underline two events that caused something else to happen.

Look for Clues: Extend Your Ideas

Circle ways that people help the Care Bags Foundation.

Ask Questions

Write a question to ask Annie Wignall.

____

____

Ask Questions: Extend Your Ideas

Write a question that you would ask someone who received a Care Bag.

____

____

Make Your Case

Put a star by the biggest reason that you feel Care Bags Foundation makes a difference.

Make Your Case: Extend Your Ideas

On a sheet of paper, write an opinion about the Care Bags Foundation. Include reasons that support your opinion.

Children read text closely to determine what the text says.

Name ______________________________

DIRECTIONS Read your revised opinion piece several times, checking for a different type of error each time. Use a colored pencil to mark your corrections. Then copy your final, edited opinion piece on the lines below.

Shades of Meaning In each pair of words, circle the word that has a more positive meaning.

1. dismissed rejected
2. spoke screamed

Children write routinely for a range of tasks, purposes, and audiences. Children practice various conventions of standard English.

Name ___________________________

Phonics

Final Syllables *-tion, -ture, -ion*

Circle a word with ***-tion, -ture,*** or ***-ion*** to finish each sentence.

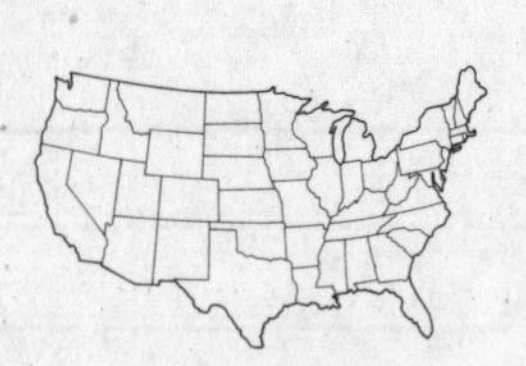

1,000,000

na**tion** mix**ture** mill**ion**

1. I saw a horse in the _____.	portion pasture
2. I watched from one _____ of the yard.	section suction
3. I moved with _____.	culture caution
4. I walked in slow _____.	motion station
5. I'd like to see a _____ horses.	million cushion

Children apply grade-level phonics and word analysis skills.

Benchmark Vocabulary

Name ______________________________

DIRECTIONS Write sentences using the words below.

liquid   ignite

Write in Response to Reading

DIRECTIONS Write a summary of the author's main purpose for writing *Alfred Nobel: The Man Behind the Peace Prize.* Use evidence from the text to support your answer.

Children demonstrate contextual understanding of Benchmark Vocabulary. Children read text closely and use text evidence in their written answers.

Name ________________________________

Writing

DIRECTIONS Identify the author's purpose for writing *Alfred Nobel: The Man Behind the Peace Prize*. Then write a paragraph that explains your opinion about the author's purpose. Use details and examples that support your opinion.

Conventions

Connections Between Words Circle words that have a connection to the word *watermelon*. Then write one sentence using both words.

1. juicy   shiny   sweet

2.

Children write routinely for a range of tasks, purposes, and audiences. Children practice various conventions of standard English.

Benchmark Vocabulary

Name ____________________

DIRECTIONS Write sentences using the words below.

startled ports

Write in Response to Reading

DIRECTIONS Reread the first paragraph on p. 126 of *Alfred Nobel: The Man Behind the Peace Prize*. What is the main topic of this paragraph? Use examples from the text to support your answer.

Children demonstrate contextual understanding of Benchmark Vocabulary. Children read text closely and use text evidence in their written answers.

Name ______________________

DIRECTIONS Revisit pp. 124–131 of *Alfred Nobel: The Man Behind the Peace Prize.* Do you think Alfred Nobel wanted to make the world safer? Explain why or why not. Use details and examples from the text to support your answer.

Children analyze and respond to literary and informational text.

Name ____________________

DIRECTIONS Write about how the topic of *Alfred Nobel: The Man Behind the Peace Prize* connects with the unit title, Changing the World. Use words from the text to support your response.

Connections Between Words Write two sentences that use connected words.

1.

2.

Children write routinely for a range of tasks, purposes, and audiences. Children practice various conventions of standard English.

Name ______________________________

Benchmark Vocabulary

DIRECTIONS Write sentences using the words below.

invention dynamite prevent

Write in Response to Reading

DIRECTIONS Reread p. 141 of *Alfred Nobel: The Man Behind the Peace Prize*. Why did Alfred believe that his invention would prevent war? Use examples from the text to support your answer.

Children demonstrate contextual understanding of Benchmark Vocabulary. Children read text closely and use text evidence in their written answers.

Writing

Name ____________________

DIRECTIONS Think about how Alfred reacted to the loss of Emil by continuing to work on making nitroglycerin safe. Write an opinion about how Alfred proceeded after the tragedy. Would you have done the same thing? Explain why or why not.

Conventions

Connections Between Words Tell how the underlined words are connected. Then write a sentence, using connected words.

1. Today we had tacos for lunch. The meat is spicy, and the tomatoes are juicy.

2.

Children write routinely for a range of tasks, purposes, and audiences. Children practice various conventions of standard English.

Name ______________________________

Benchmark Vocabulary

DIRECTIONS Write sentences using the words below.

will estate

Write in Response to Reading

DIRECTIONS Reread pp. 142–149 of *Alfred Nobel: The Man Behind the Peace Prize*. Do you think Alfred would have created The Nobel Prizes if he had not read his obituary? Use evidence from the text to support your answer.

Children demonstrate contextual understanding of Benchmark Vocabulary. Children read text closely and use text evidence in their written answers.

Name ______________________________

DIRECTIONS Draft a letter to the editor in response to the editorial that your class wrote. Decide whether you agree or disagree with the opinion presented in the editorial. Include reasons to support your opinion.

Connections Between Words Write sentences using the words below. Then briefly explain the connection between the words.

Alfred Nobel   life   inspirational   famous

Children write routinely for a range of tasks, purposes, and audiences. Children practice various conventions of standard English.

Name ________________________________

Benchmark Vocabulary

DIRECTIONS Write sentences using the words below.

terribly escape

Write in Response to Reading

DIRECTIONS Reread pp. 150–151 of *Alfred Nobel: The Man Behind the Peace Prize*. How do you think Alfred would feel about the list of Nobel Peace Prize winners? Use details from the text to support your answer.

Children demonstrate contextual understanding of Benchmark Vocabulary. Children read text closely and use text evidence in their written answers.

Name ________________________________

DIRECTIONS Revisit *Alfred Nobel: The Man Behind the Peace Prize* and select one cause-and-effect relationship. Then write a paragraph that explains what happened and why. Use specific details from the text to support your answer.

Children analyze and respond to literary and informational text.

Name ______________________

Writing

DIRECTIONS Write a paragraph that expresses an opinion about how Alfred's invention impacted communities. Use linking words and phrases to connect your opinions and reasons. Remember to clearly state your opinion at the beginning of your paragraph.

Conventions

Connections Between Words Write two sentences that use words connected with the word *legacy*.

Children write routinely for a range of tasks, purposes, and audiences. Children practice various conventions of standard English.

Name ______________________________

Suffixes *-ness, -less, -able, -ible*

Add ***-ness, -less, -able,*** or ***-ible*** to each word to make a word from the box.
Write the new word on the line.

affordable	fearless	fitness	goodness
reversible	terrible	thankless	useless

1. afford ____________	**2.** fit ____________
3. thank ____________	**4.** fear ____________
5. good ____________	**6.** use ____________

Pick a word from the box to match the clue.
Write the word on the line.

7. has two sides you can use: ____________

8. very bad, something feared: ____________

Children apply grade-level phonics and word analysis skills.

Name ______________________________

Benchmark Vocabulary

DIRECTIONS Write sentences using the words below.

accomplishment legacy

Write in Response to Reading

DIRECTIONS Reread pp. 148–151 of *Alfred Nobel: The Man Behind the Peace Prize*. How do the text features in this section connect with Alfred's dream of making the world safer for people? Use details from the text to support your answer.

Children demonstrate contextual understanding of Benchmark Vocabulary. Children read text closely and use text evidence in their written answers.

Name ______________________________

DIRECTIONS Reread pp. 146–148 of *Alfred Nobel: The Man Behind the Peace Prize*. Write an opinion about Alfred Nobel's will from the point of view of one of his family members. Use persuasive words to support your opinion. Remember to provide a strong concluding statement.

Use Root Words to Identify Unknown Words Write sentences using words with the root words *sleep* and *develop*.

1. ______________________________

2. ______________________________

Children write routinely for a range of tasks, purposes, and audiences. Children practice various conventions of standard English.

Name ______________________

Benchmark Vocabulary

DIRECTIONS Write sentences using the words below.

awkward serious

Write in Response to Reading

DIRECTIONS Reread pp. 173–175 of *A Picture Book of Eleanor Roosevelt*. How does the information in this section relate to the main purpose of the text? Use details from the text to support your answer.

Children demonstrate contextual understanding of Benchmark Vocabulary. Children read text closely and use text evidence in their written answers.

Name ______________________________

DIRECTIONS Identify the author's purpose for writing about Eleanor Roosevelt. Then list four pieces of evidence from the text that support the author's purpose.

Author's Purpose: ______________________________

Text Evidence: ______________________________

Children analyze and respond to literary and informational text.

Name ______________________________

Writing

DIRECTIONS Write a paragraph that gives Eleanor Roosevelt a new honorary title. Revisit the text for ideas. Remember to support your choice with strong reasons from the text, and explain why you believe she deserves the new title.

Conventions

Use Root Words to Identify Unknown Words Write sentences using words with the root words *invent* and *command*.

1. ______________________________

2. ______________________________

Children write routinely for a range of tasks, purposes, and audiences. Children practice various conventions of standard English.

Name ______________________________

DIRECTIONS Write a sentence using the word below.

pure

DIRECTIONS Reread p. 156 of *A Picture Book of Eleanor Roosevelt*. What reasons does the author provide to support the claim that Eleanor missed her father terribly? Use evidence from the text to support your answer.

Children demonstrate contextual understanding of Benchmark Vocabulary. Children read text closely and use text evidence in their written answers.

Name ______________________________

Wanted: Great Student Leaders!

Do you have lots of school spirit and fun ideas for helping your school? Are you a good leader? Then you may belong on the student council!

Many schools have student councils. These are groups of students who are chosen to share ideas and make decisions about student activities. Students often elect student council members in a class or grade-level election. Council members work hard to be good students, good citizens, and good examples to everyone at school.

Some students are officers with special duties. They lead the council meetings, keep records, and work with school staff members. Others are representatives. They talk to the students in their classes to get ideas. Later, they report back to the class about decisions the student council has made.

But what does a student council actually do? It might organize an event, such as a school carnival. It might raise money for new equipment. It might plan volunteer activities, such as a food drive, to help people in the community. If there is a problem in the school, the student council may discuss possible solutions to the problem.

Are you ready to make a difference in your school? If so, the student council may be the place for you!

Children read text closely to determine what the text says.

Name ______________________________

Look for Clues

Underline text clues that help you understand what a student council does.

Look for Clues: Extend Your Ideas

Circle what council members work hard at.

Ask Questions

Write a question that you might ask students that are on a student council.

____

Ask Questions: Extend Your Ideas

Write a question to ask of a student running for student council.

____

Make Your Case

Put a star above a sentence that helps you understand the author's main purpose.

Make Your Case: Extend Your Ideas

On a sheet of paper, list two personality traits you think a student council member should have.

Children read text closely to determine what the text says.

Name ______________________

Writing

DIRECTIONS Write a list of facts from the text that support Eleanor's opinion that boarding school was a good place. Remember to only include facts from her life that support why she felt that way.

Conventions

Identify Root Words Write a sentence using the root word for each word shown below.

difference   discovery   accomplishment

1.

Children write routinely for a range of tasks, purposes, and audiences. Children practice various conventions of standard English.

Name ______________________________

DIRECTIONS Write a sentence using the word below.

stricken

DIRECTIONS Reread the second paragraph on p. 161 of *A Picture Book of Eleanor Roosevelt*. How does the word *hated* impact the text? Use examples from the text to support your answer.

Children demonstrate contextual understanding of Benchmark Vocabulary. Children read text closely and use text evidence in their written answers.

Name ________________________

DIRECTIONS Using evidence from the text, answer the following questions about *A Picture Book of Eleanor Roosevelt*.

1. Reread p. 165. Describe how the phrase "paid little attention" impacts the text?

2. Reread p. 167. What does the word *refused* tell you about Eleanor Roosevelt?

3. Reread pp. 168–169. List several words and phrases from this section that help to explain Eleanor Roosevelt's importance to Franklin Delano Roosevelt.

Children analyze and respond to literary and informational text.

Writing

Name ______________________________

DIRECTIONS Why do you think the author chose to write about Eleanor Roosevelt? Revisit *A Picture Book of Eleanor Roosevelt* to look for clues about the author's purpose. Then develop a plan for your opinion paragraph.

Conventions

Identify and Use the Prefix *re-* Write sentences using words with the prefix *re-*.

1.

2.

Children write routinely for a range of tasks, purposes, and audiences. Children practice various conventions of standard English.

Name ______________________________

Benchmark Vocabulary

DIRECTIONS Write sentences using the words below.

rights minorities

Write in Response to Reading

DIRECTIONS Reread pp. 172–176 of *A Picture Book of Eleanor Roosevelt*. What key ideas and details support the idea that Eleanor Roosevelt was "First Lady of the World." Use evidence from the text to support your answer.

Children demonstrate contextual understanding of Benchmark Vocabulary. Children read text closely and use text evidence in their written answers.

Name ______________________________

DIRECTIONS Write a paragraph that explains a connection between Eleanor Roosevelt's actions and one of the historical events listed on the time line on p. 182. Use evidence from the text to show the connection.

Children analyze and respond to literary and informational text.

Name ______________________________

Writing

DIRECTIONS Write a draft of your opinion piece about why you think the author chose to write about Eleanor Roosevelt. Revisit *A Picture Book of Eleanor Roosevelt* to look for clues about the author's opinion. Use your list of key ideas and details from the previous lesson to support your writing.

Conventions

Dictionaries Reread pp. 172–182 of *A Picture Book of Eleanor Roosevelt*. Find one unfamiliar word and look it up in a dictionary. Then write a sentence using the word.

Children write routinely for a range of tasks, purposes, and audiences. Children practice various conventions of standard English.

Name ______________________________

Prefixes *micro-, mid-, mis-, non-*

Read the clues.
Write micro-, mid-, mis-,
or **non-** to finish the words.

microscope **mid**air
misplace **non**fat

1. middle of the week __________ week	2. an error __________ take
3. true story __________ fiction	4. act badly __________ behave
5. peaceful __________ violent	6. about July 1 __________ year
7. an error in printing __________ print	8. something that makes sound louder __________ phone
9. makes no sense __________ sense	10. a wrong act __________ deed

Children apply grade-level phonics and word analysis skills.

Name ______________________________

Benchmark Vocabulary

DIRECTIONS Write sentences using the words below.

invention stricken

Write in Response to Reading

DIRECTIONS Revisit *Alfred Nobel: The Man Behind the Peace Prize* and *A Picture Book of Eleanor Roosevelt*. What did Eleanor Roosevelt and Alfred Nobel have in common? Use details from both texts to support your answer.

Children demonstrate contextual understanding of Benchmark Vocabulary. Children read text closely and use text evidence in their written answers.

Name ______________________

Writing

DIRECTIONS Think of ways to make your opinion piece about Eleanor Roosevelt stronger. Add reasons and examples to support your opinions. Revise your conclusion to make it stronger. Revisit the text to look for additional reasons and examples.

Conventions

Use Dictionaries Revisit *A Picture Book of Eleanor Roosevelt* to find two words you do not know. Use a dictionary to find the meaning of each word.

1. ______________________

2. ______________________

Children write routinely for a range of tasks, purposes, and audiences. Children practice various conventions of standard English.

Name ______________________________

Benchmark Vocabulary

DIRECTIONS Write sentences using the words below.

legacy pure

Write in Response to Reading

DIRECTIONS Revisit p. 148 of *Alfred Nobel: The Man Behind the Peace Prize* and p. 178 of *A Picture Book of Eleanor Roosevelt.* What do these sections tell you about how Alfred and Eleanor felt about world peace? Use examples from both texts to support your answer.

Children demonstrate contextual understanding of Benchmark Vocabulary. Children read text closely and use text evidence in their written answers.